William Murphy

William Murphy

Geometric Concepts in Islamic Art

Issam El-Said and Ayşe Parman

Foreword by Titus Burckhardt

 World of Islam Festival Publishing Company Ltd

World of Islam Festival Publishing Company Ltd., London

First published 1976
ISBN 0 905035 03 8

Published and produced by the World of Islam Festival
Publishing Company Ltd., London.

Designer: Colin Larkin
Editor: Caroline Montagu

Set in 12/13 pt Monophoto Plantin 110
Printed on 115 gsm Blade coated cartridge
Monochrome origination: Westerham Press
Filmset by Westerham Press and printed in England by
Westerham Press Ltd., Westerham, Kent.

Acknowledgements

We are indebted to Dr Esmat El-Said for her encouragement and constructive criticism of this work. The photographs are by:
Alistair Duncan, Robert Harding, Robert Harding Associates, Antony Hutt, John Knight-Smith, Ronald Lewcock, Roland Michaud, A. O. Remeyes, and the following Museums have been of great assistance:
British Museum, Victoria and Albert Museum.

Jacket photograph of Issam El-Said © Harlip.

List of Plates

Contents

Transliteration

The Muslim and Christian calendars

Readers should note that whenever dates are given in the form, for example, 246/860, the first date is reckoned on the Muslim calendar (the basic date of which, the Hijira, corresponds to A.D. 622), and the second on the Christian calendar.

References

The references following each chapter should be read in conjunction with the detailed bibliography at the end of the book.

Arabic Letter	Transliteration
ء	'
ب	b
ت	t
ث	th
ج	j
ح	ḥ
خ	kh
د	d
ذ	dh
ر	r
ز	z
س	s
ش	sh
ص	ṣ
ض	ḍ
ط	ṭ
ظ	ẓ
ع	'
غ	gh
ف	f
ق	q
ك	k
ل	l
م	m
ن	n
و	w
ه	h
ة	t
ي	y

Short Vowels

ـَ	a
ـُ	u
ـِ	i

Long Vowels

ـَا	ā
ـُو	ū
ـِي	ī

Diphthongs

ـَوْ	aw
ـَيْ	ay
ـِيّ	iyy
ـُوّ	uww

Persian Letters

پ	p
چ	ch
ژ	zh
گ	g

Foreword

This book by Issam El-Said and Ayşe Parman throws much light on an aspect of Islamic art which is little known and rarely studied but which is none the less fundamental. It is true that the use of particular geometric schemas as a basis of composition is not the exclusive prerogative of Islamic art, for it is found to a greater or lesser extent in all traditional art, in the West no less than in the East, and this principle shines out as clearly in the windows of Gothic cathedrals as it does in the *mandalas* that lie at the root of sacred architecture in India. But it is in Islamic art that this 'sacred geometry' is developed with the greatest inner logic and amplitude. This means that Islamic art is far less a way of expressing emotion than a science and that a Muslim artist will willingly subordinate his individuality to the, as it were, objective and impersonal beauty of his work.

Europeans of our day are distrustful of any canon that is imposed upon art and they are all too ready to regard it as an obstacle to 'creativity', especially when this canon can be translated into mathematical formulae. Now the geometric models used in traditional art have nothing to do with a rational, or even a rationalistic, systematization of art; they derive from a geometry which is *a priori* non-quantitative and which is itself creative because it is linked to data inhering directly in the mind. At the basis of this geometry there lies the circle which is an image of an infinite whole and which, when it is evenly divided, gives rise to regularly shaped polygons which can, in their turn, be developed into star-shaped polygons elaborated indefinitely in perfectly harmonious proportions.

Issam El-Said and Ayşe Parman are careful to trace the use of these geometric patterns back to the very earliest methods used in architecture for the measurement of space. In fact, in the absence of exact units of measurement, it was possible to transpose a plan from one scale to another by reference to a geometric pattern inscribed within a 'guiding circle' of variable size. A large circle would be traced out by means of a cord on the site of the proposed building and, after the division of this circle into a fixed number of segments, the geometric figure which had served as the outline for the original plan would then be superimposed upon it. Now the important thing from an aesthetic point of view is the qualitative, and non-quantitative, nature of such a procedure in which the implicit presence of the circle guarantees a harmonious relation between the parts and the whole. Once this framework had been laid down, the artist could place within it the various elements of the work in hand, giving full play to his imagination which was thus guided but not suffocated; a perfect rule inspires, it does not deaden.

In the Islamic perspective, this method of deriving all the vital proportions of a building from the harmonious division of a circle is no more than a symbolic way of expressing Tawhīd, which is the metaphysical doctrine of Divine Unity as the source and culmination of all diversity. It is not surprising, therefore, that Muslim artists should have explored all the geometric systems that depend upon the regular division of the circle. In its purest form, this geometrical 'speculation' can be seen in the art of decoration, whether this be ornamentation in ceramic mosaics or a relief covering the surface of a dome.

The science of proportions doubtless goes back to remote antiquity and even to prehistory. Moreover, there is an analogy to proportion in the realm of metre, namely rhythm and, again, in music, in the form of the interval. From another point of view, rhythm is involved indirectly in the visual order; it governs in particular the flow of the arabesque. Lastly, proportion and rhythm come together to determine the art of Arabic calligraphy, which plays a leading role in the world of Islam.

Islamic art has been extensively studied in relation to its history; but the study of its artistic methods, which comprise both a science and craftsmanship, has been broached by only a few enquiring minds. Issam El-Said and Ayşe Parman's book provides a starting-point for investigation of this latter category. More than that, it contains a message which is in singular contrast to a certain modern conception of art which is assessed by purely psychological and subjective criteria. The traditional science of proportion affirms, in short, that beauty is not a matter of traditional taste; whilst having unlimited possibilities, it has laws; it is objectively true.

Titus Burckhardt
Fez
October, 1975

Introduction

The aim of this study is to trace man's approach to measure and to outline the geometric concepts of composition and the process of their application in the different fields of Islamic art.

Most fields of Islamic art are linked from China to Spain by a unifying concept of composition despite the diversity of materials, forms or styles used.

Representational art did not have priority in the Islamic culture. This caused the development of a unifying concept of composition in abstract decorative art, which transcends the physical world rather than presenting a pictorial imitation of nature. In other civilizations the canons of representational art, based on subjective aesthetics, prevented the achievement of a similar unifying abstract concept between the visual arts and other forms of artistic expression.

The following chapters are an attempt to explain how geometry was employed as a method for mensuration and composition before the appearance of our present numerical decimal system in the eighth century A.D. A brief explanation is also presented on how in conceptual terms most forms of artistic expression in the Islamic civilization were founded on the same ordering principle or *mīzān* (balance, order), which was conceived as the basis of the laws of creation.

Through the geometric approach to design, the systematic execution of decorative arts, calligraphy, architecture and the composition of music and Arabic poetry were unified. The geometric method enabled the artists to create freely yet easily and correctly without the restrictions of a numerical system. Perfect inter-relationships between the parts and the whole of the composition were attained irrespective of mode, form or scale of expression. Hence a universality was achieved in the Islamic world which is consistent with the Islamic belief that all creations are harmoniously inter-related.

The Islamic heritage is an important link in the chain of man's progress and in the assimilation of the Mesopotamian and Ancient Egyptian heritage and of the Asiatic and Greek culture. Its significant contributions in the fields of science have been recognized, but its achievements in the field of art and design have been greatly underestimated.

Chapter I
Man and Measure

1 Historical Background

There is evidence of the existence in the Near East, some time during the fourth millennium B.C., of two societies each with an entirely different structure: the Mesopotamian state-cities and Egypt united under the rule of a divine king. These societies had developed systems of government, a social order, private ownership, commerce, etc., which depended on accepted systems to organize, codify and record them. By 3000 B.C. in both regions there were calendrical astronomers, surveyors, architects and irrigation engineers who based their work on a mathematical foundation. Sumer and Egypt both produced monumental modes of artistic expression (e.g. temples, palaces, sculpture, etc.), which were without precedent. These innovations are important markers of the transformation of prehistoric cultures into the first great civilizations.

The architectural feats of Mesopotamia and Egypt encourage us to suppose that they had elaborate rules of mensuration. The Egyptian rope-stretchers and temple surveyors must have developed a reproducible method, by using peg and cord, to trace circles and straight lines on sand. This enabled them to establish a geometric procedure for generating precise and accurate constructions of a particular style such as the Great Pyramid at Jizah, built about 2600 B.C. It is only fitting here to emphasize how considerable was the debt of Greek geometry to both Egypt and Mesopotamia. The Greek genius was to transform geometry into an exact abstract reasoning device. The culmination of their contribution, which moulded geometry into an academic form, was achieved by Euclid, the founder of the Alexandrian School about 300 B.C., in his book, *The Elements*. This illustrates the evolution of the common human heritage, and shows how successive civilizations borrowed from preceding ones and developed methods of self-expression that best served their particular beliefs and practices.

2 Measuring and Dividing Dimensions

It has been argued justifiably that necessity motivated man to construct the implements and dwellings best suited to his mode of survival, and that trial and error established the reproducible methods employed in the process, and hence the 'traditional' skills.

Until the eighth century A.D., when the introduction of the zero and the decimal system by the Arabs from their origins in India took place, and the use of Arabic numerals from one to nine was established, the abstract mathematical operational value of numbers as we understand them today did not exist. Before that time, each number was symbolized by a mark or sign to denote its qualitative value. At a later stage, the alphabet was substituted for these marks, e.g., the Ancient Greek, Roman, Hebrew or Arabic (Abjad Hawaz) alphabet, as a system for counting. These letters were used in basic calculations and did not have great mathematical operational value. To illustrate this, let us try and divide:

$$\frac{XXXII}{IV} \text{ or } \frac{ﻟﺐ}{ﺩ} \left(\text{or } \frac{32}{4} \right)$$

Hence, to presume any linear scale unit for measure based on a numerical system such as a metre, or a foot with decimal subdivisions and multiples, could not have been conceived without the zero. Complicated calculations without the aid of such a system would have been impossible.

It could be argued that man used a more practical and simple approach for solving such problems. If a man were given a length of rope, etc., he could use any convenient unit, e.g., his hand, arm, foot or stride, as a unit measure to state its dimension. Then, irrespective of the dimension, he could divide it into two or more equal parts simply by folding the given length into 2, 3, 5, etc., equal folds. Any number of further proportional divisions could be achieved by the repeated folding into two. Thus the required number of unit parts is obtained by folding in half and thereby doubling the number of the previous fold (Figure 1).

UNIT LENGTH

$\frac{1}{2}$ FIRST FOLD $\frac{1}{3}$ $\frac{1}{5}$

$\frac{1}{4}$ SECOND FOLD $\frac{1}{6}$ $\frac{1}{10}$

$\frac{1}{8}$ THIRD FOLD $\frac{1}{12}$ $\frac{1}{20}$

Figure 1

Number of parts in first fold
    2, 3, 5, etc.
Number of parts in second fold
    4, 6, 10, etc., respectively
Number of parts in third fold
    8, 12, 20, etc., respectively

    The result in divisions by the folding technique would always be in whole units, and thus fractions would not be involved. This method is still employed at present in various Asiatic and African societies.

3 The Organization of Space

    Once again, we can obtain clues from a 'traditional' technique in current use to explain how this organization of space could have been achieved. In the construction of geometric patterns in some traditional Islamic crafts (e.g., wood inlaying, metalwork, ceramic designs) the compasses and ruler are the only two major instruments used. In principle, this method is reminiscent of the rope-stretching techniques of surveying, using peg and rope for a pair of compasses, in the planning of buildings in Ancient Egypt. Man has found through the utilization of geometry (meaning literally land measure), based on the circle, a perfect method to shape areas without resorting to complicated mathematical calculations such that, after the development of mathematics (the decimal system), this method, complete in itself, remained unaltered.

    From a circle it is possible to generate any regular polygon once the circumference is divided equally to the required number of sections and straight lines join these points of division. It will be illustrated below how, through using the three basic divisions of the circumference into 3, 4 or 5 equal sections, the rest of the most commonly used polygons are obtained.

To construct an equilateral triangle with side AB

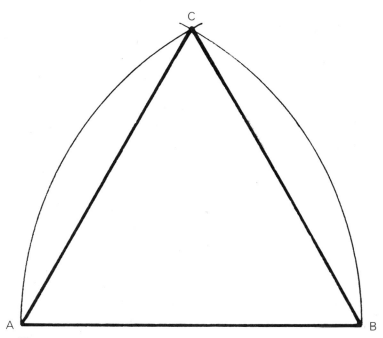

Figure 2

Draw line AB (Figure 2).
With centre A and radius AB describe an arc above the line.
Repeat same radius with centre B, such that the two arcs intersect at C.
Draw straight lines from C to A and C to B.

To construct a square with side AB

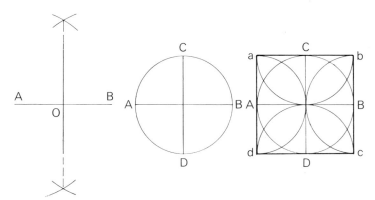

Figures 3a, b and c

Bisect AB at O (Figure 3a).
With centre O and radius OA describe a circle cutting the bisecting perpendicular at C and D (Figure 3b).
With the same radius OA draw four semi-circles with centres at A, B, C and D respectively (Figure 3c).
Join in straight lines the points of the intersecting semi-circles a, b, c and d to form the square.

To construct a pentagon within a circle

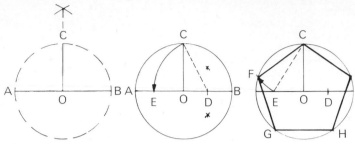

Figures 4a, b and c

With centre O and radius OA describe a circle cutting the upper perpendicular at C (Figure 4a). Bisect radius OB at D (Figure 4b).
With centre D and radius DC draw an arc cutting OA at E.
With centre C and radius CE draw an arc cutting the circumference at F (Figure 4c).
FC equals one side of the inscribed pentagon CFGHI.
With centre F and radius CF, cut the circumference at G. Repeat with centres G, H and I successively. C, F, G, H, I is then the required inscribed pentagon.

To construct a hexagon with side AB

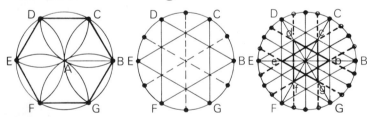

Figures 5a, b and c

Describe a circle with radius AB. The radius of the circle cuts its circumference into six equal parts forming the hexagon BCDEFG (Figure 5a).
Further equal division to 12, 24, etc., can be achieved simply by joining alternated points of the hexagon by straight lines making two equilateral triangles BDF and CEG which form a six-pointed star BCDEFG (Figure 5b). Further point-joining with straight lines through the centre of the circle of the opposite points of the intersecting sides of the star, and extending these lines to cut the circumference will give twelve subdivisions of the circumference. Draw diameters DG, CF and BE. Join points of intersection b, c, d, e, f, g of diameters with sides of triangles and extend them to cut the circumference into 24 equal parts (Figure 5c).

It is the geometric possibility of the radius being employed to subdivide the circumference of the circle it describes into 6, 12, 24, etc. equal sections that encourages one to believe that this was probably the basis of the Sumerian and Babylonian sexagecimal system of measure, and that it is related to the astrological system of twelve signs of the Zodiac, the calendrical divisions of the year into twelve months, and of measure based on six, such as the dozen or the carat.

The initial divisions of the circumference of the circle into 3, 4 or 5 equal parts can be carried out geometrically (as explained above). The

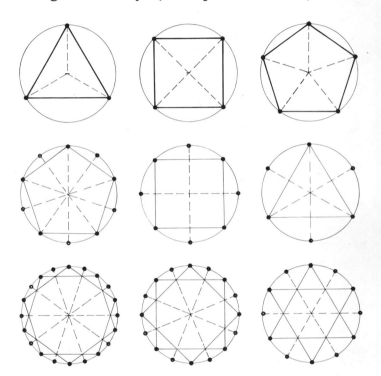

Figure 6

middle line of Figure 6 shows how, by bisecting the sides of the inscribed polygon, the subdivisions of the circumference are doubled to 6, 8 and 10 equal parts respectively. By using the point-joining method the subdivisions of the circumference can be increased by a factor of two (see bottom line in Figure 6) whereby the initial divisions are redoubled to 12, 16 and 20 equal parts. Thus the subdivision of the circumference of a circle by triangulation and the point-joining method is in principle similar to the subdivisions of any linear dimension by the folding technique. The regular polygons of 3, 4, 5, 6, 8, 10, 12, 16 and 20, etc., sides are obtained by joining the points of division on the circumference with straight lines.

These regular polygons can be subdivided to basic units in the shape of right-angled triangles, the number of these triangular sub-units being equal to twice the number of sides of the comprising polygon (Figure 7). The sides of these triangular sub-units consist of the radius of the circle circumscribing the polygon, the bisecting perpendicular line from the centre to the side of the polygon and one-half of the side of the polygon.

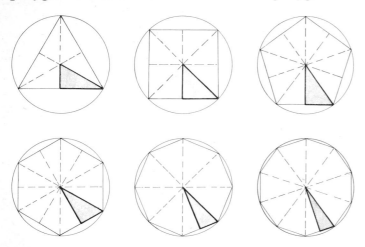

Figure 7

From this we can observe that the basic triangular sub-units of all the polygons with a common circumscribing circle differ only in the proportion of their two perpendicular sides. Hence, possibly, comes the notion that 'the triangle is to geometry as one is to numbers'. It is this constant relationship of the parts to each other, which we described as proportion, which determines the shape and properties of regular geometric forms irrespective of size.

4 Proportion

The concept of proportion is based on ratio. 'Ratio is the relation between two things of the same kind, of which we know the measure of the one as compared with the other. We call a man father when we contrast him to his child, and the latter a child when comparing with the father. Similarly, we call one thing half of another which is double of the former.'[1] Ratio is expressed as a:b or represented as a fraction $\frac{a}{b}$, where a and b can be any number. Proportion is the equality of two or more ratios which can be either:

continuous: e.g., $\frac{a}{b} = \frac{b}{c} = \frac{c}{d}$ etc.,

$$\frac{2}{4} = \frac{4}{8} = \frac{8}{16} \text{ etc.}$$

or discontinuous: e.g., $\frac{a}{b} = \frac{c}{d} = \frac{f}{g}$ etc.,

$$\frac{2}{4} = \frac{3}{6} = \frac{5}{10} \text{ etc.}$$

Both have a constant characteristic ratio, in this case represented numerically as $\frac{1}{2}$.

The rectangle is the most commonly used shape in design. Its characteristic ratio is expressed by the measure of its short side (a) to its long side (b); a:b can be any ratio, 2:3, 3:5, 5:6, 5:8 (Figure 8).

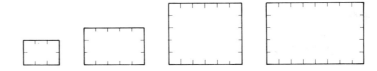

Figure 8

In a square, a and b are equal, and therefore the proportion is $\frac{a}{b} = \frac{1}{1} = 1$, i.e., unity. When constructing a rectangle the short side (a) of which is the side (a) of a square and the long side (b) is equal to the diagonal of that square, the ratio a:b is equal to $1 : \sqrt{2}$ (from the theorem of Pythagoras) (Figure 9).

Figure 9

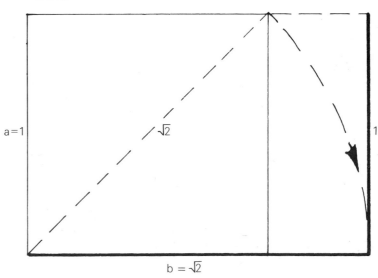

The square root of two, $\sqrt{2}$, is called an irrational number because there is no rational number which, when multiplied by itself (squared), gives two. Therefore its approximate value will lie between two numbers one small and the other large,

i.e. 1.4	and 1.5
1.41	and 1.42
1.414	and 1.415
1.4142	and 1.4143
etc.	etc.

This led to the doctrine of the incommensurable which simply means that in theory the side and the diagonal of a square cannot be measured exactly using the same scale. In other words $1 : \sqrt{2}$ is not expressible as the ratio of two integers.

The Greeks could not explain the meaning of $\sqrt{2}$ because they had no numerical system, as we have demonstrated above with the aid of the decimal system. The irrational numbers $\sqrt{2}$, $\sqrt{3}$, $\sqrt{5}$, etc., were called by the Pythagoreans the 'unspeakable numbers' which could be drawn but not expressed numerically.

Rectangles with the ratio of their two sides $a : b$ equal to $1 : \sqrt{2}$, $1 : \sqrt{3}$, $1 : \sqrt{5}$, etc., i.e., $1 :$ 'irrational number', were called by Hambidge[2] 'the dynamic rectangles', the construction of which is illustrated in Figure 10.

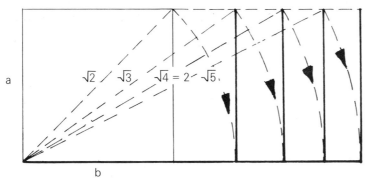

Figure 10

'Symmetria' in classical terminology meant the proportionality between the constituent elements of the whole. Since the concepts of 'symmetria' are based on harmonic proportions, the linear numerical methods of analysis of geometrically constructed designs invariably result in approximations or inaccuracies because of the irrational numbers derived from the proportions of the geometric elements of the design.

References

1. Al-Bayrūnī, p. 11.

2. Ghyka, M., p. 6.

Chapter II
Geometric Patterns in Islamic Design

1 The Concept of the Repeat Unit

To our knowledge, no record has survived to instruct us in the theory of designing Islamic geometric patterns. In this chapter, we will attempt to illustrate how the craftsmen at different times and places in the Muslim world proceeded to apply the geometric principles to the practical problems of making geometric patterns. Although others[1] have tried to describe the construction of these patterns, their works involved incomplete or unsatisfactory explanations. In our opinion, these works lack the fundamental concept of what we will call the 'repeat unit' of a design. It is the systematic arrangement of the repeat unit which produces the overall design.

In the Muslim world today, the craftsmen engaged in making geometric patterns on wood, marble, metal, ceramics, etc., employ the traditional tools of compasses and rule. The geometric method, applied, developed and perfected by unknown masters of the past, is no longer a device for generating new designs, but one for reproducing the old.

In the following sections of this chapter, detailed illustrations will show how the shape of the repeat unit of a design is determined by use of a circle. The basic or unit measure is taken as the radius. The initial divisions of the circumference of the circle (described by the unit radius) into 4, 6 or 5 equal sections (or multiples of these sections) determine the system of proportioning used to generate the repeat unit of the design. Although the analyses of the repeat units based on 7, 9, 11 (etc.)-sided regular polygons and their stars, or combinations of these polygons, have not been included, the principles of their construction are the same as those described in this book.

2 The Square and the Root Two System of Proportion

This section includes all designs based on the repeat pattern generated from squares inscribed in a circle. The repeat pattern, which gives the design its character, is determined by grid lines drawn between points established by the intersecting sides of the squares inscribed in the circle. By inscribing squares within the circle, a geometric method of proportional subdivision of the area of the repeat unit and, thereby, of all the grid lines of the pattern, is achieved.

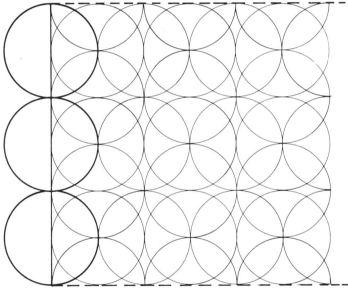

Figure 11a

Figure 11b

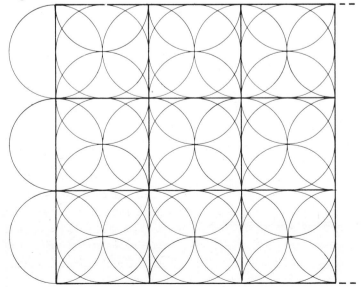

When a surface is to be decorated, one of its sides is divided equally into a number of parts corresponding to the number of repeat units required. The area is then filled with circles (Figure 11a), the diameters of which are equal to the subdivisions of the side of the surface being decorated. The area is now equipartitioned into square repeat units by the point-joining method (Figure 11b). This procedure is similar to the method of constructing a square as described on page 3.

In each square repeat unit (Figure 12a) the proportion of the side of the inscribed square ACBD to the side of the circumscribed square abcd is $\frac{AD}{ad} = \frac{1}{\sqrt{2}}$ (i.e., ad = AB, the diagonal of the inscribed square). Thus the sides of the series of concentric squares drawn in Figure 12b are related by the proportion $1 : \sqrt{2}$, and therefore the areas are progressively halved. In Figure 12c where only the squares of Figure 12b with vertical and horizontal sides are considered, the proportion of the sides of these series of squares is $1 : 2$ which means that the sides are progressively halved and the areas quartered.

In Figure 13a by drawing the diagonals ac and bd of the circumscribed square and joining their points of intersection with the circle we form the square efgh, which is congruent to square ACBD, but with sides parallel to square abcd. The squares ACBD and efgh thus create an octagonal star, which we refer to as the 'master grid' of the unit pattern based on this octagonal star. By drawing the concentric octagonal stars (Figure 13b) using the point-joining method we establish a geometric system of harmonious subdivision of the repeat unit. In this system of concentric squares the consecutive parallel sides (Figure 13c) are related in the proportion of $1 : \sqrt{2}$ and the alternate parallel sides are related in the proportion of $1 : 2$; therefore all the sides and the diagonals of the square repeat unit can be subdivided in these proportions. This illustrates the best practical geometrical system of mensuration which was available when arithmetical calculations were not possible.

It was mentioned in the introduction that the geometric method allows the artist great scope for improvisation. The designs presented on pages 44 to 47 illustrate how a square repeat unit can be modified to a rectangular repeat unit; this allows for new repeat patterns and the incorporation of variations into a basic design. Alternatively, the basic square shape of the repeat

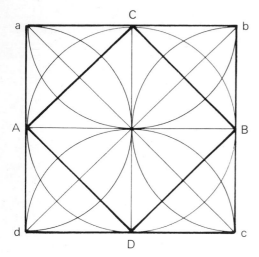
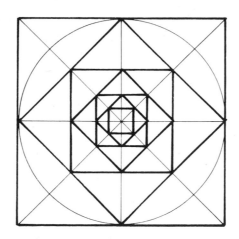
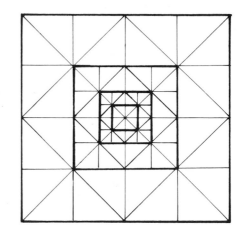

Figures 12a, b and c

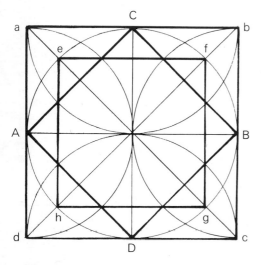

Figures 13a, b and c

unit is maintained, but the basic repeat pattern generated on a given set of grid lines is shifted as illustrated in Figure 36 (p. 49) to create variations on the original design. These modifications were especially useful in the decoration of borders.

The repeat unit of the design could be applied with the aid of a full-scale template pierced with holes at the principal intersections of the grid lines to indicate with points the lines to be drawn to generate the repeat pattern. In the working of mosaics the dimensions, shapes and the required number of component geometric forms could be accurately determined with the construction of a

single repeat unit. In lattice woodwork the repeat units could constitute the structural components as well as the decoration of the whole.

On pages 10 to 49 Islamic geometric designs based on the octagonal star (or the $\sqrt{2}$ system of proportioning) are analysed in the manner described. The top line of the figures shows how the master grid and the dependent grid lines of the pattern are constructed to draw the repeat pattern. Below these the overall design is given by the multiple presentation of this repeat pattern. Photographs, where they are available, show the application of the design.

Plate 1. Masjid-i-Jāmi, Farūmad, Iran, 7th/13th* century.
*see page viii for explanation

Figure 14

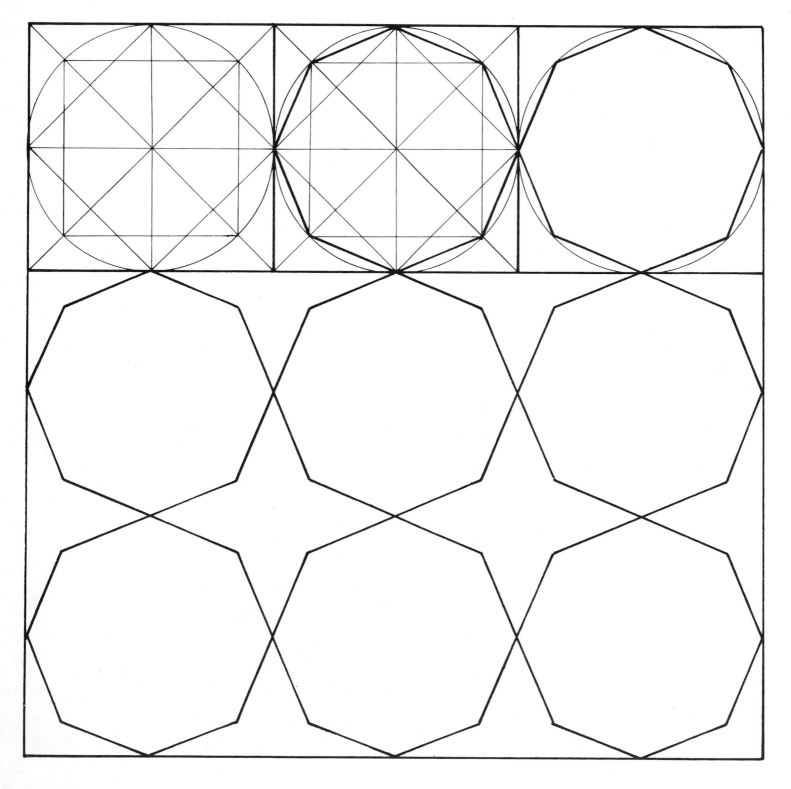

Plate 2. Wooden door from Sarij Madrasah, Fez, Morocco, 8th/14th century.

Plate 3. Masjid-i-Jāmi, Varamīn, Iran, 8th/14th century.

Plate 4. Tiles, Iran Bastān Museum, Tehran, Iran.

Figure 15

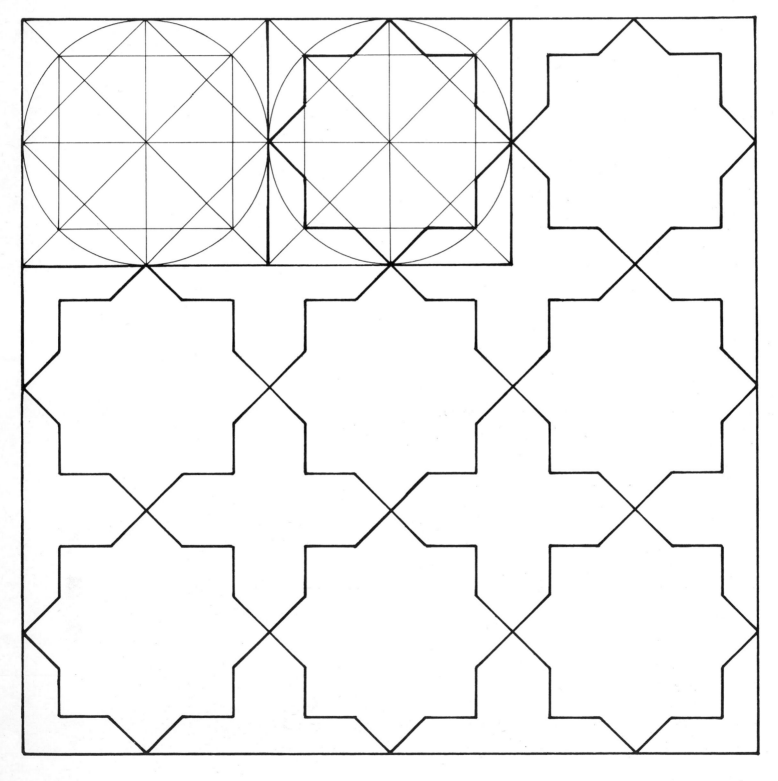

Plate 5. Taj Mahal, Agra, India, 11th/17th century.

Figure 16

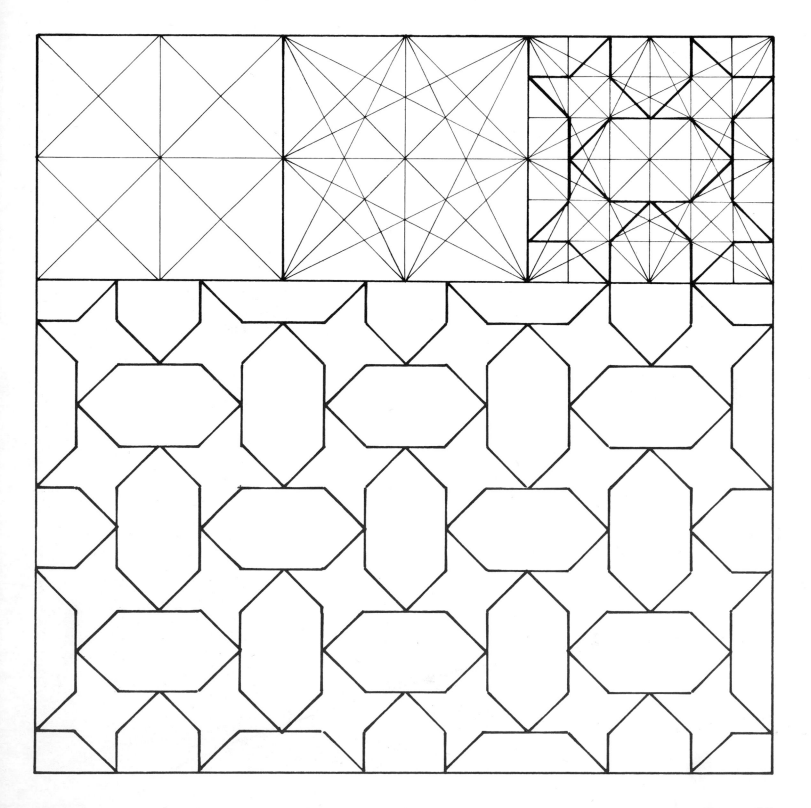

Plate 6. Portal, Büyät Karatay Madrasah, Konya, Turkey, 649/1251.

Plate 7. Tomb towers, Kharraqān, Iran, 459/1067.

Figure 17

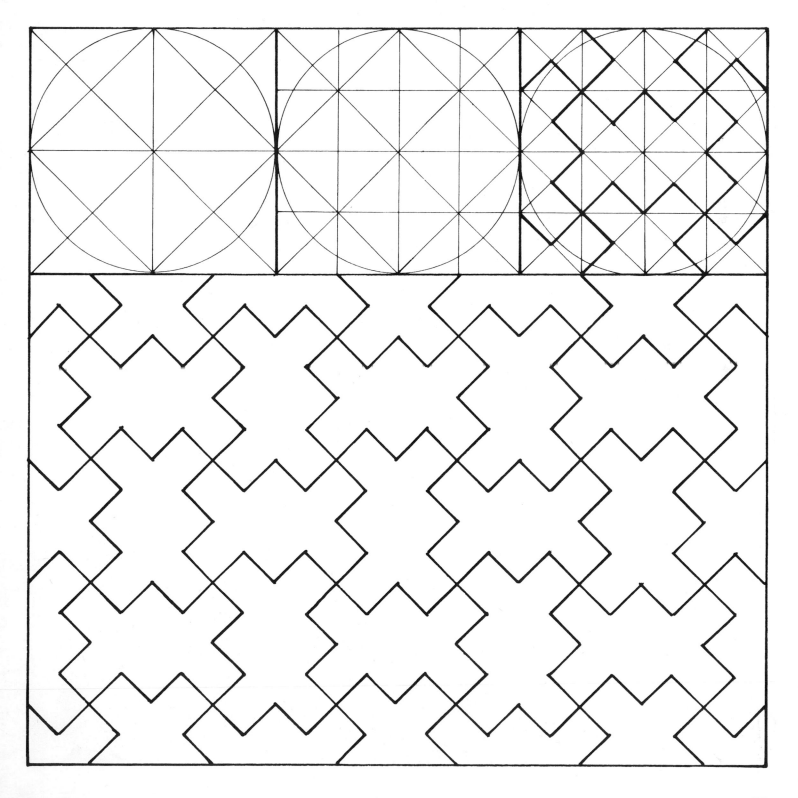

Plate 8. Tomb towers, Kharraqān, Iran, 459/1067.

Figure 18

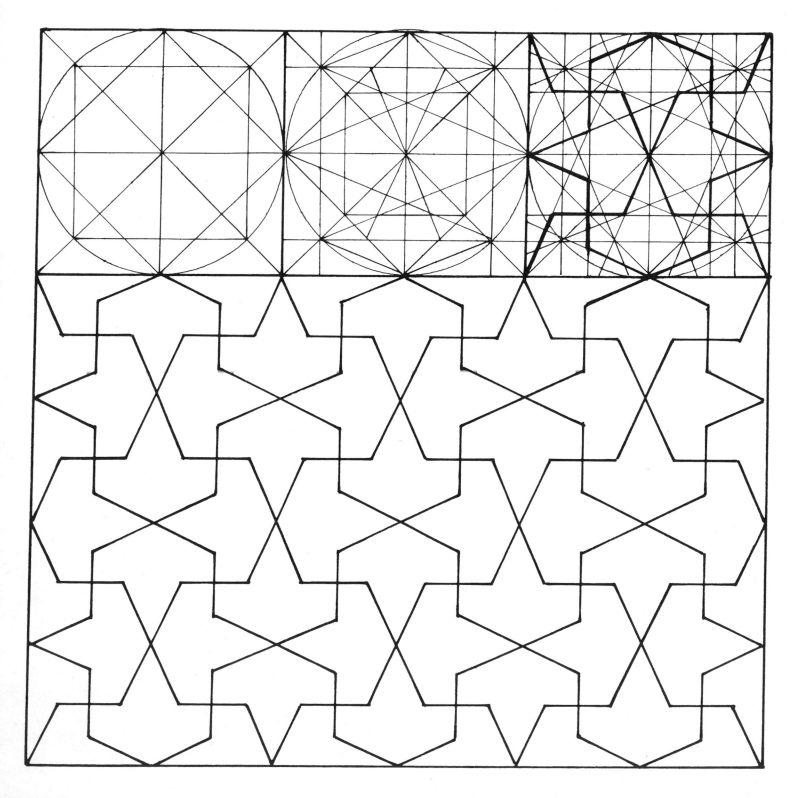

Plate 9. Minaret, Jām, Afghanistan, 7th/13th century.

Figure 19

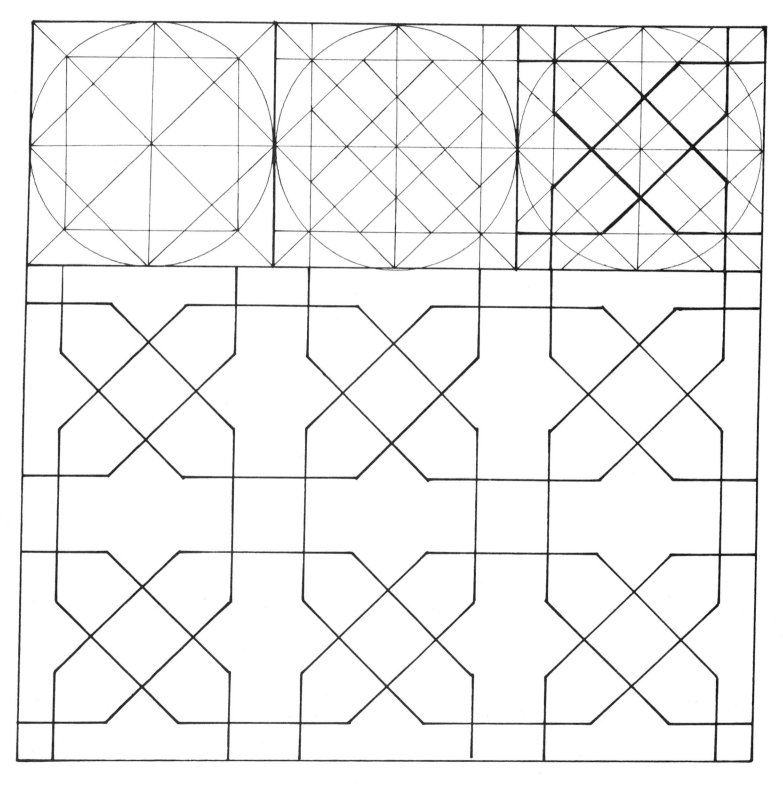

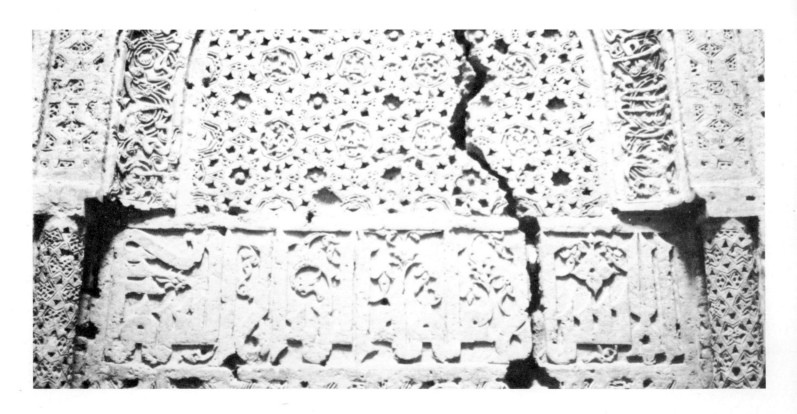

Figure 20

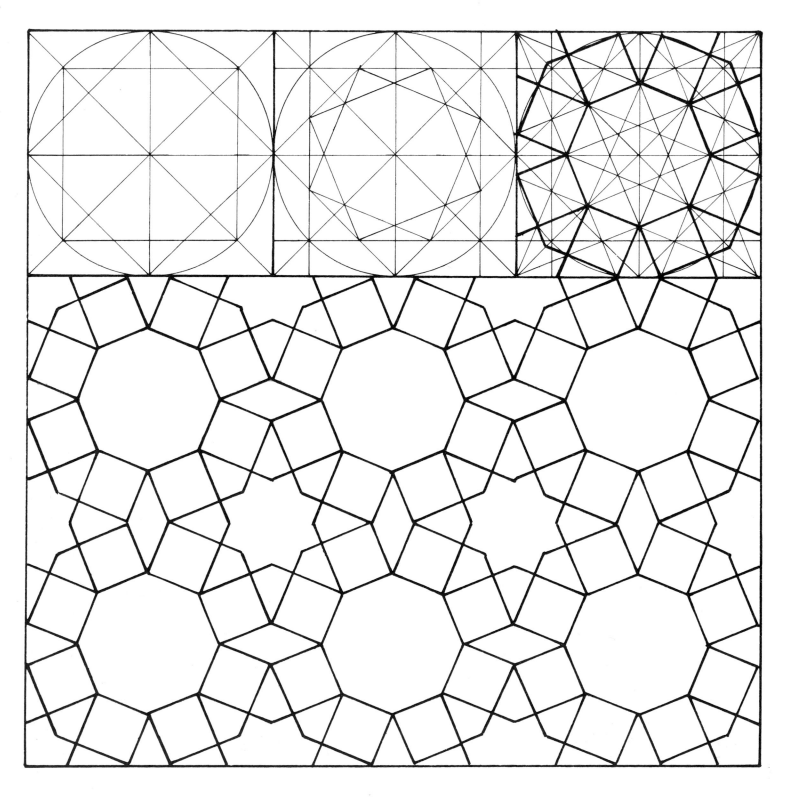

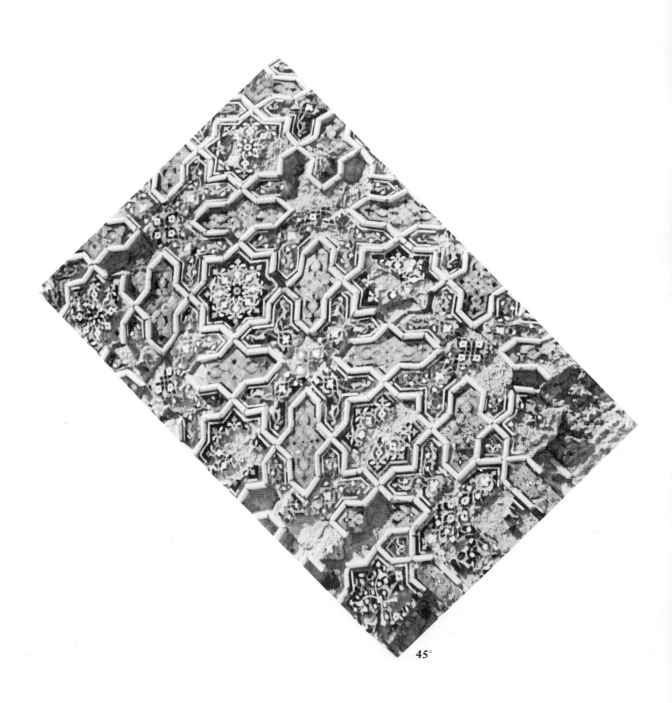

45°

Figure 21

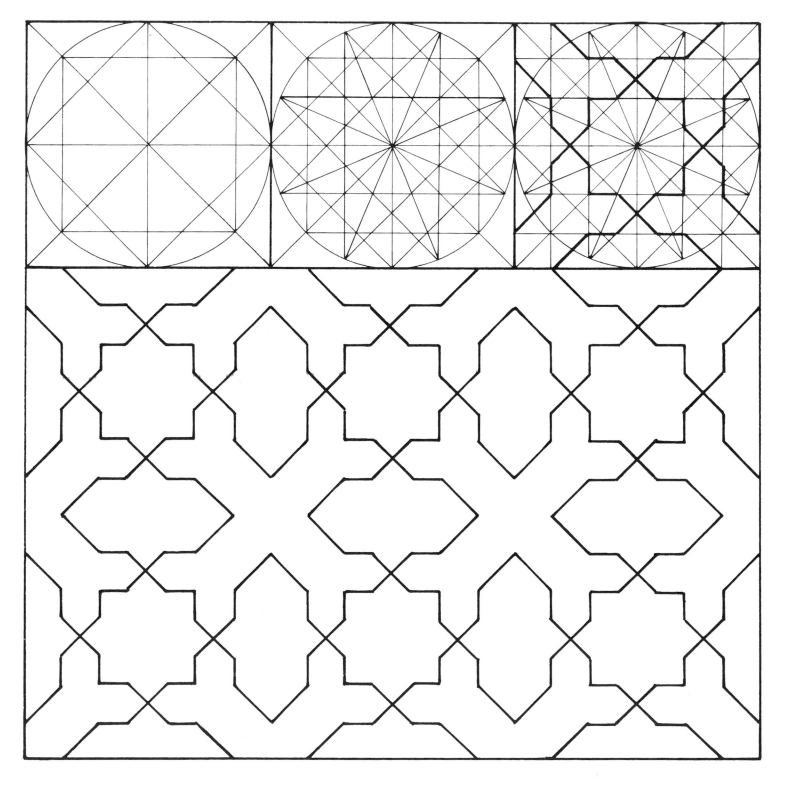

Plate 12. Carved stucco from Rayy, Tehran Museum, Iran, 5th–6th/11th–12th century.

Figure 22

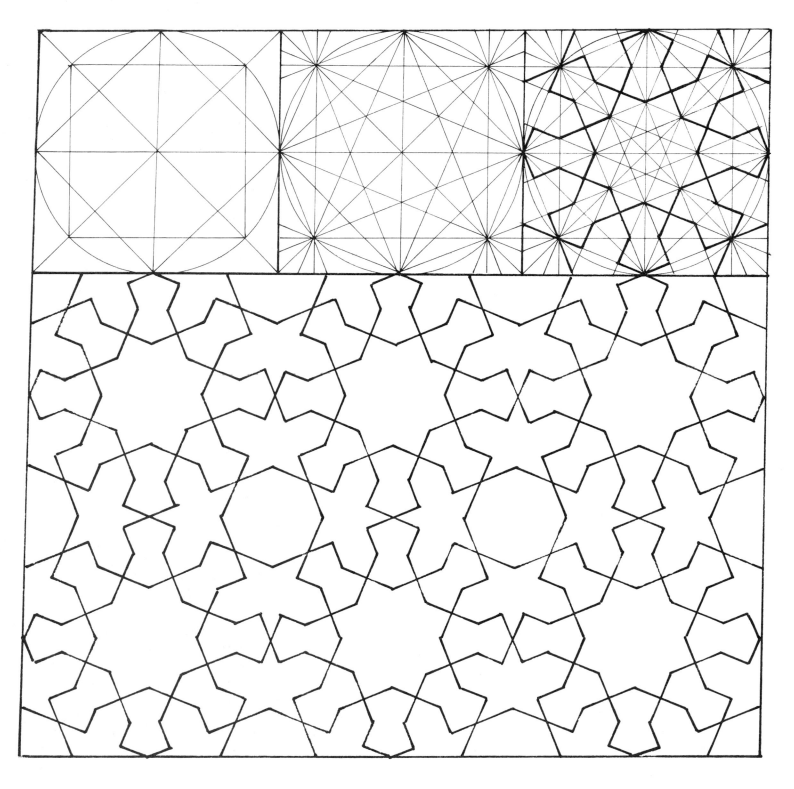

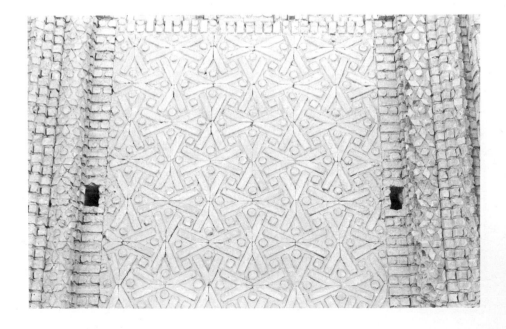

Plate 13. Tomb towers, Kharraqān, Iran, 459/1067.

Figure 23

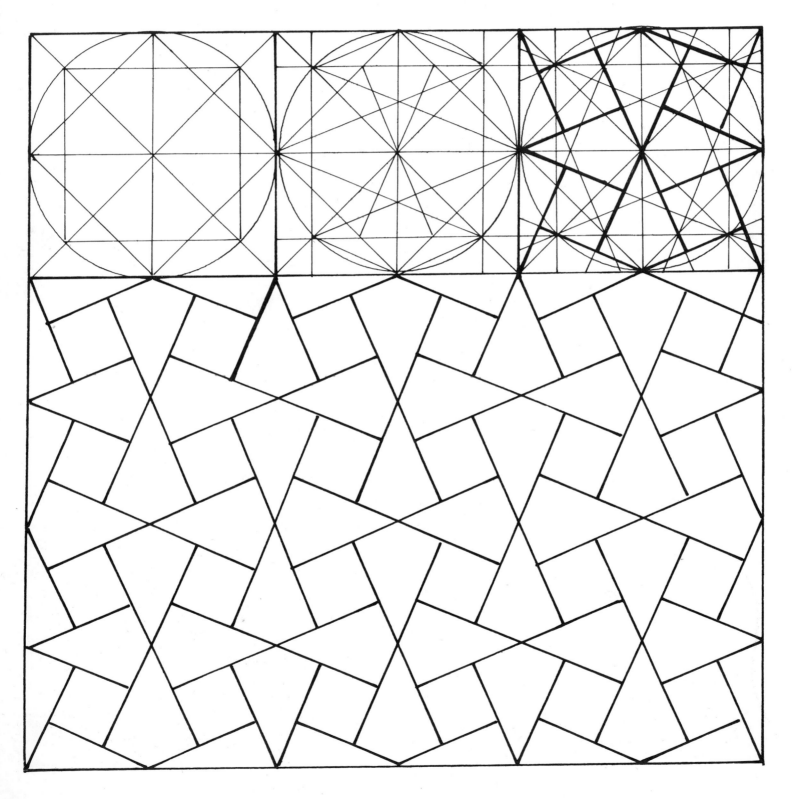

Plate 14. Mausoleum of I'timād al-Dawla, Agra, India, 1037/1628.

Figure 24

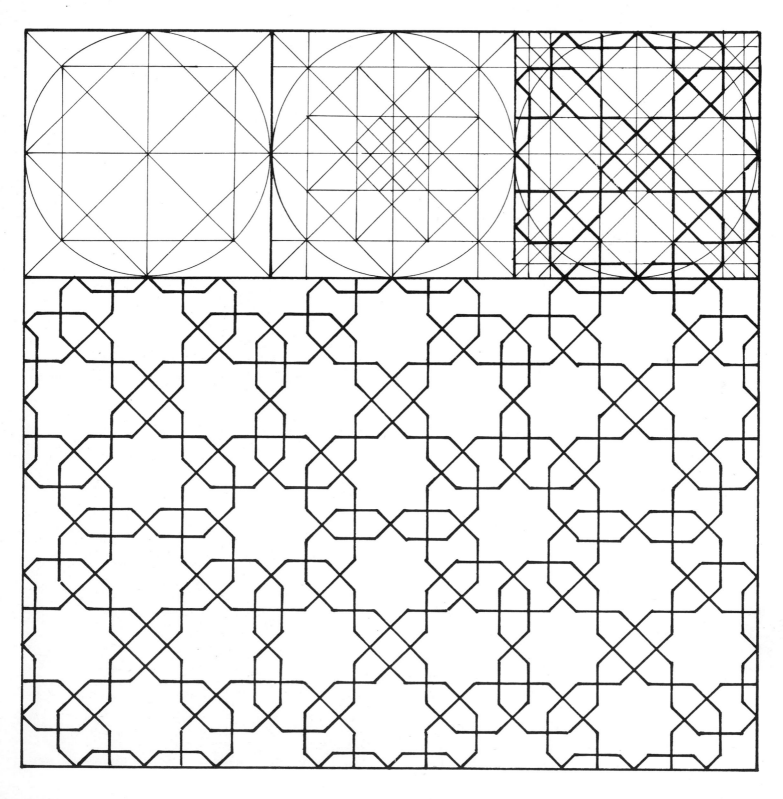

Plate 15. Madrasah, Khargird, Iran, 848/1444.

Figure 25

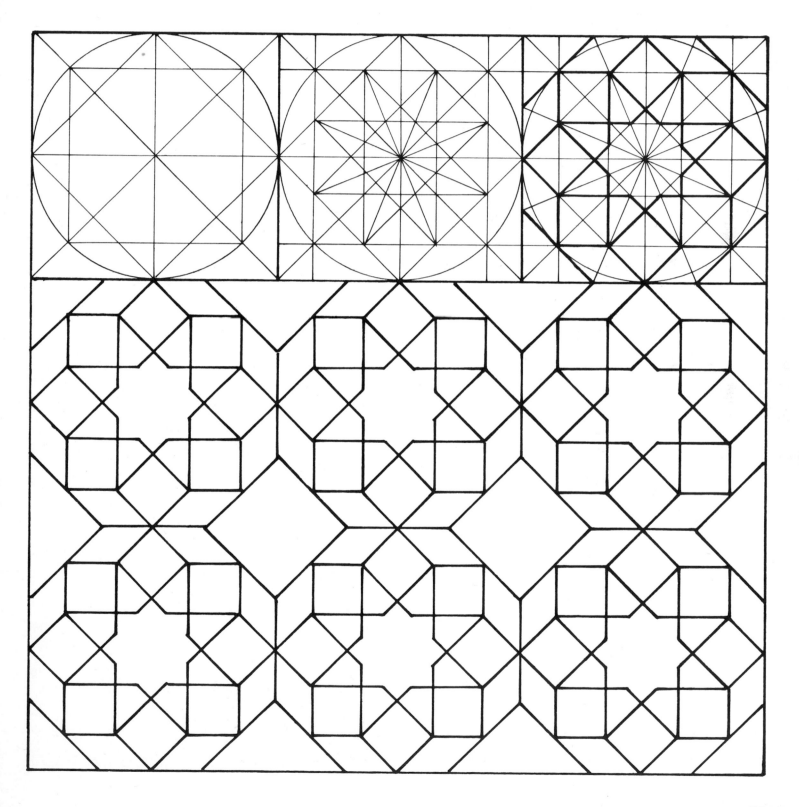

Plate 16. Telmout Castle, Morocco.

Figure 26

Figure 27

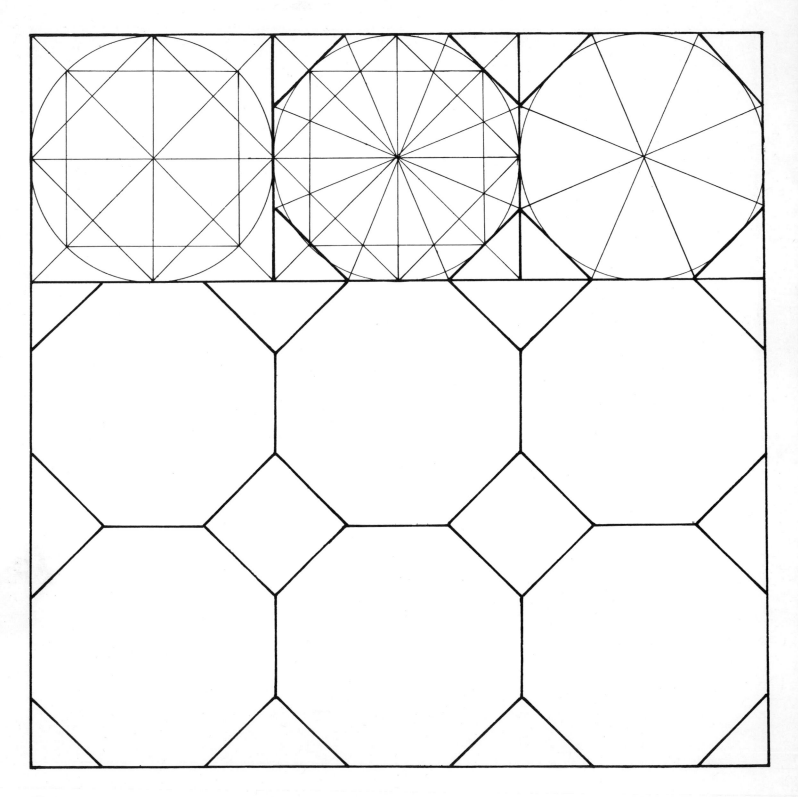

Figure 28

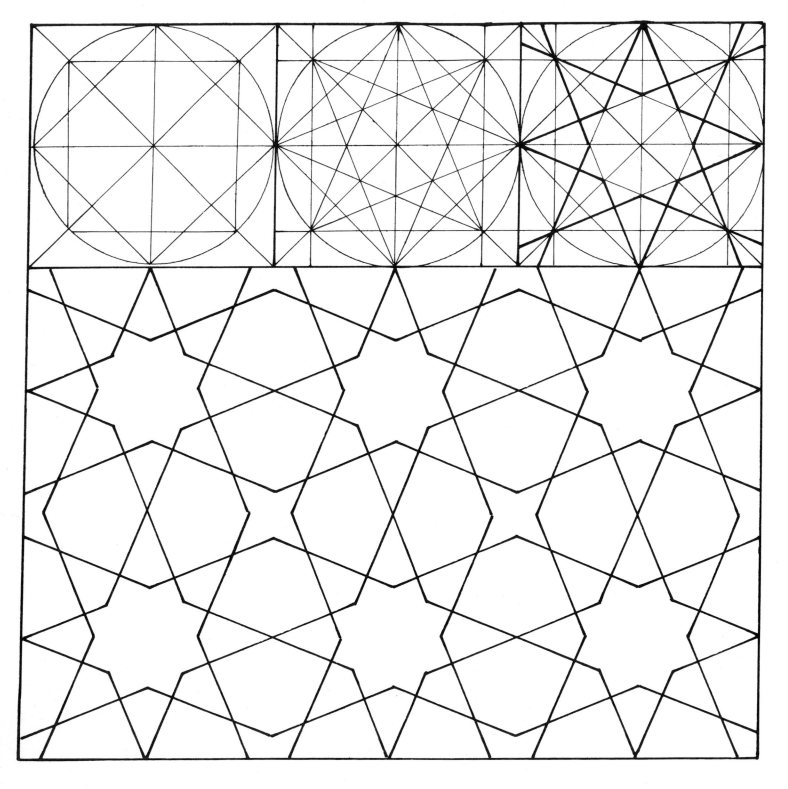

Figure 29

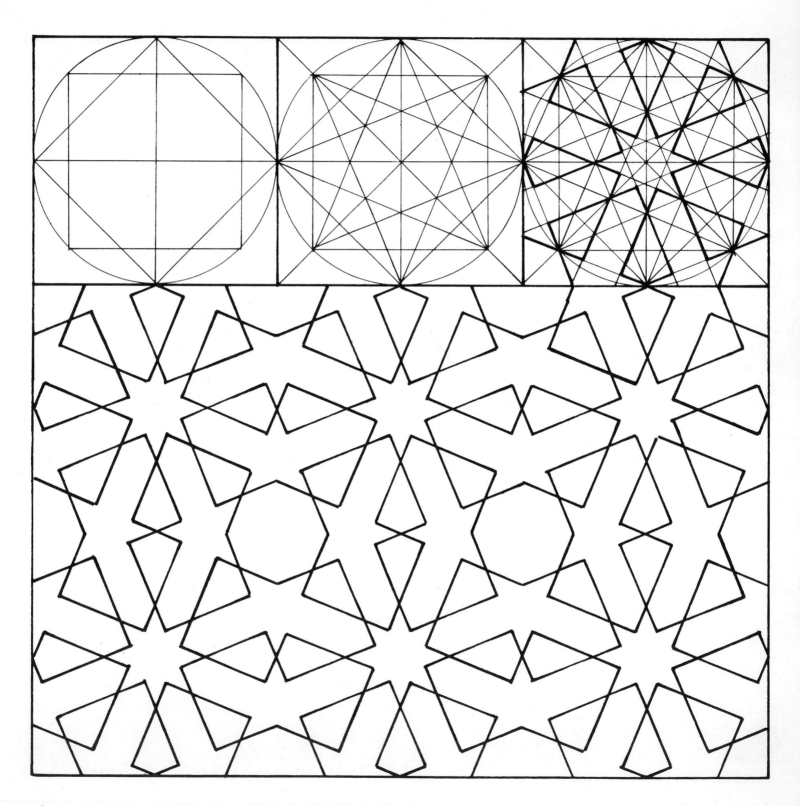

Figure 30

Figure 31

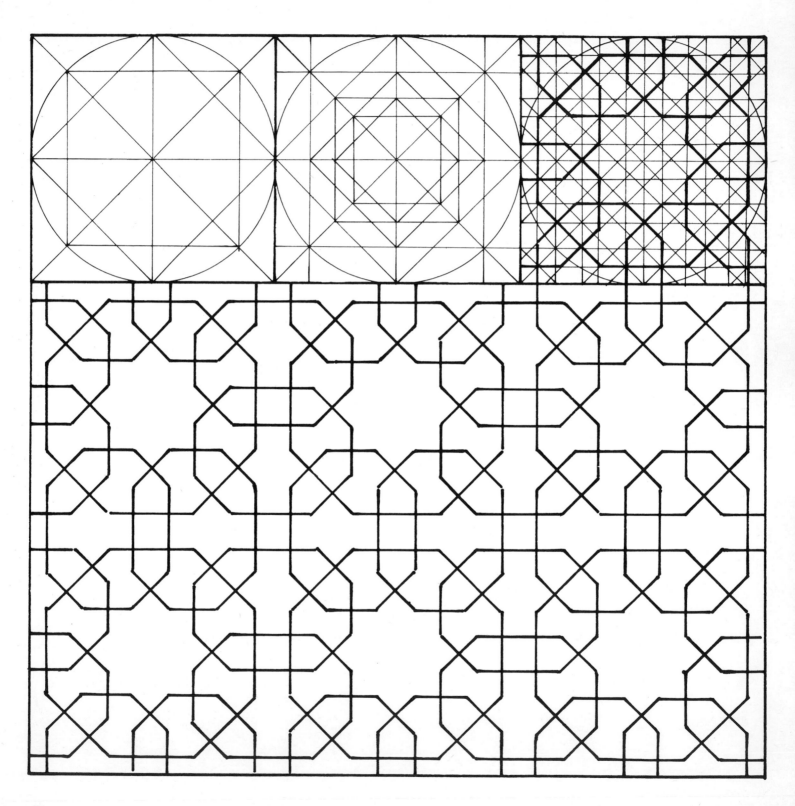

Figure 32

Figure 33

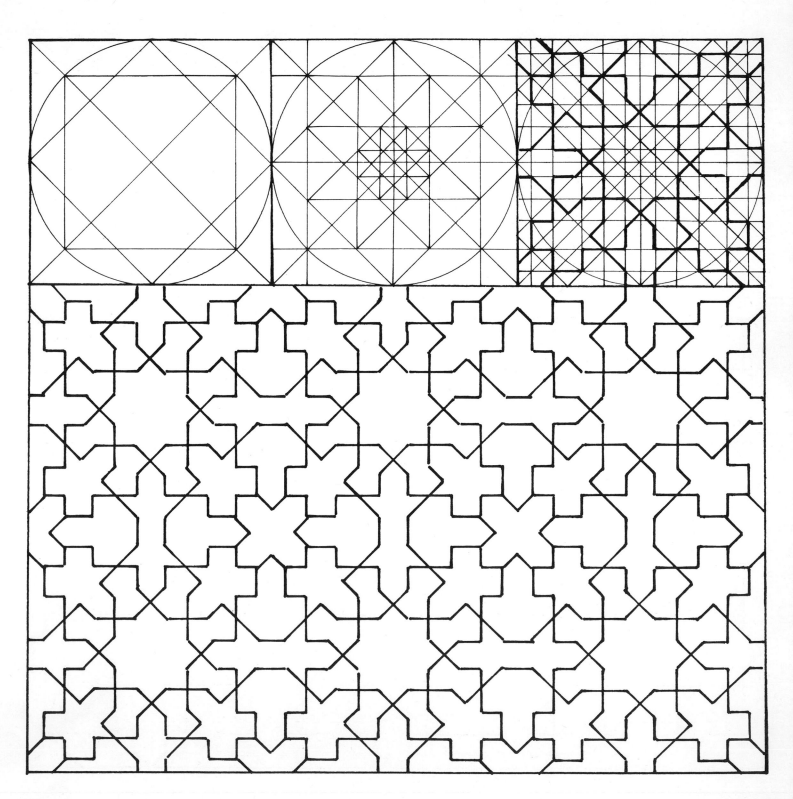

Figure 34

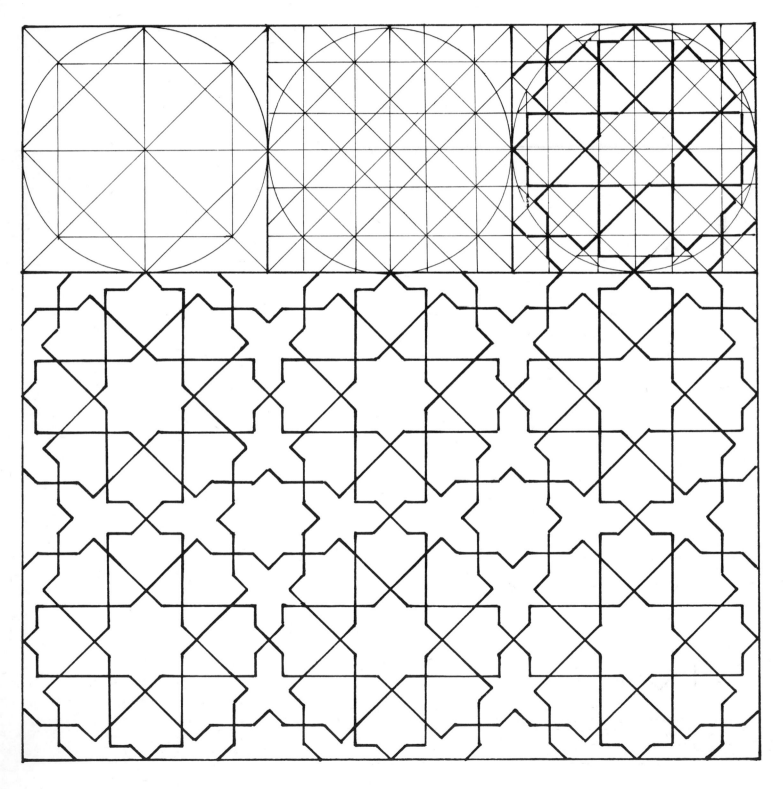

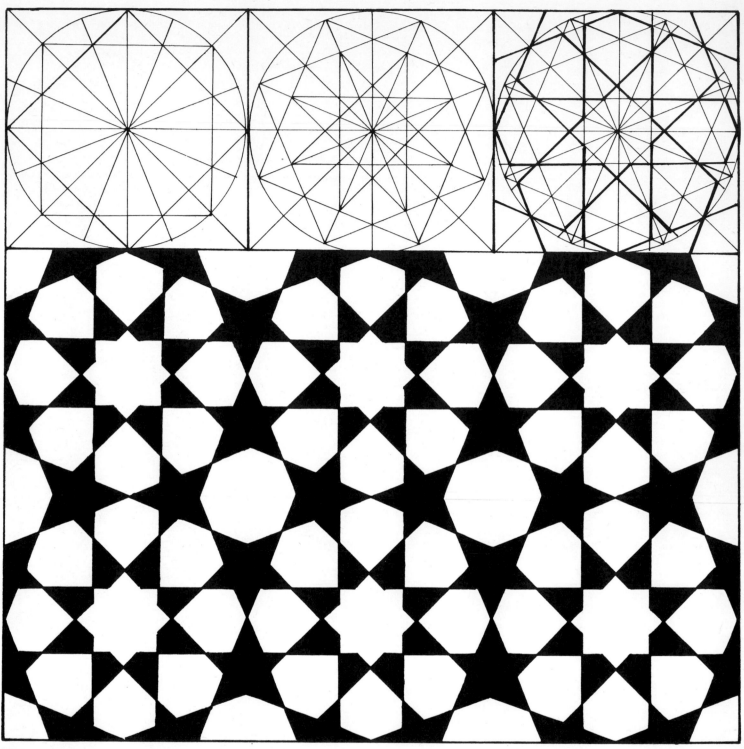

35a

Figures 35a, b, c and d. Figure 35a presents a design based on the octagonal star. The repeat unit of this design is a square with side a, which can be changed into a rectangle of sides a and b where the ratio of a:b can be equal to $1:\sqrt{2}$, $1:1+\sqrt{\frac{2}{2}}$, or to $1:1+\sqrt{2}$ as shown in Figures 35b, 35c and 35d respectively. The variations introduced into the basic design are indicated in Figures 35b and 35c. In Figure 35d, the modification of the repeat unit has resulted in the lateral shifting of the basic octagonal star repeat pattern within the consecutive horizontal bands.

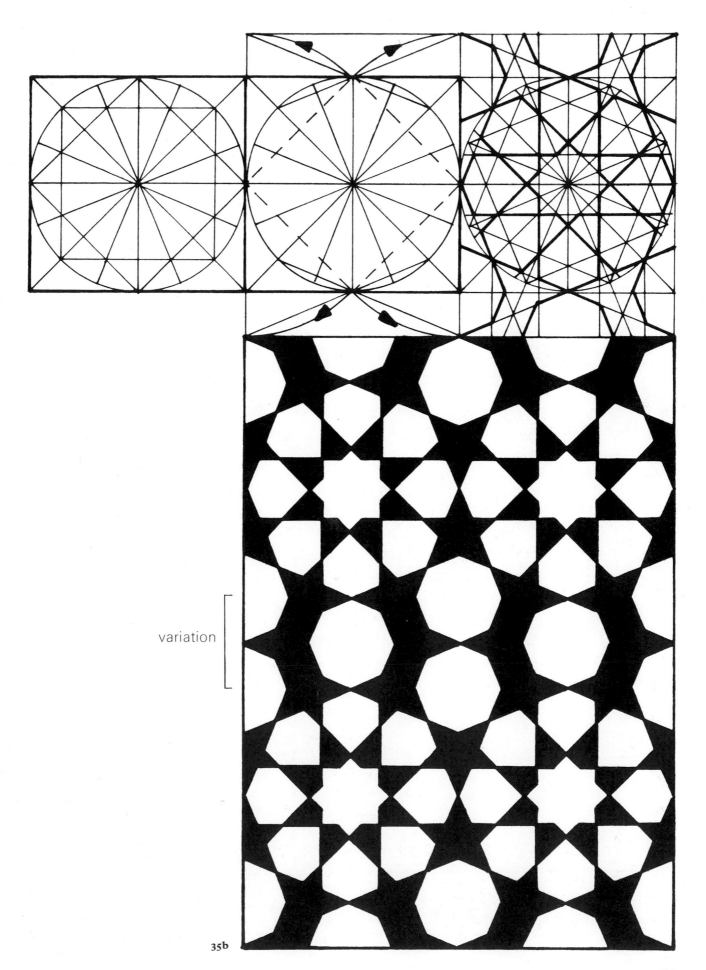

variation

35b

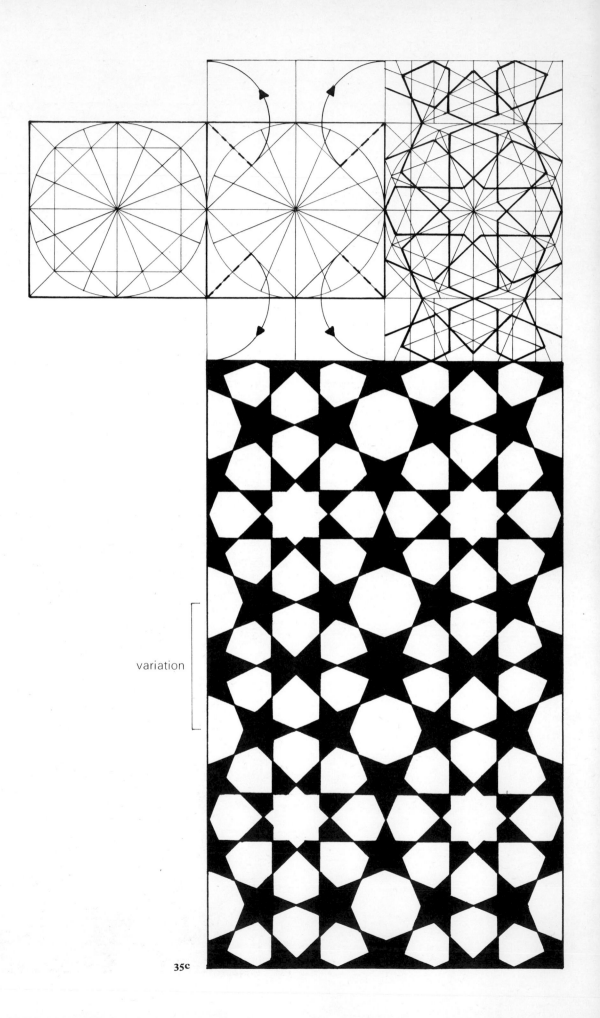

variation

35c

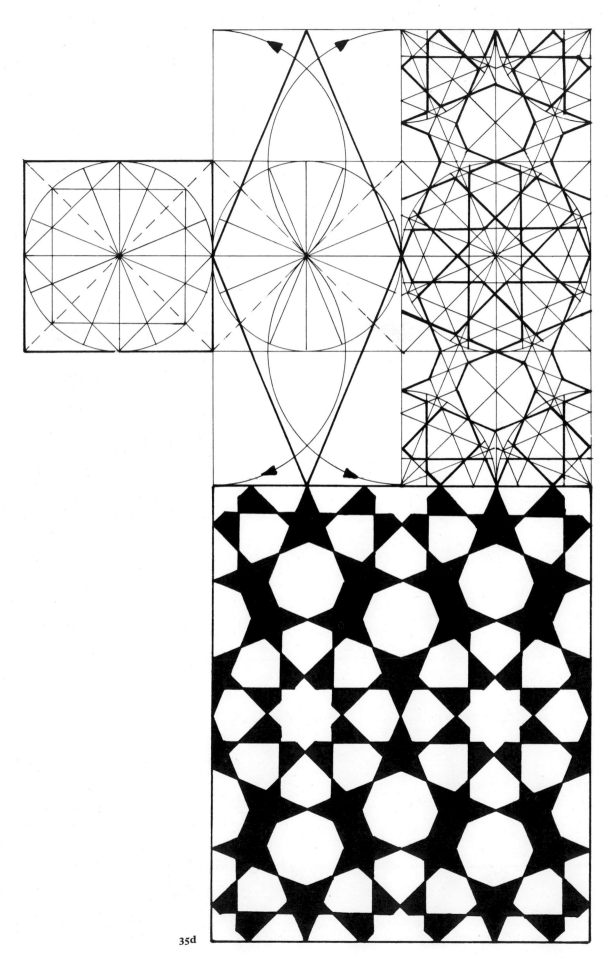

35d

a

b

c

48

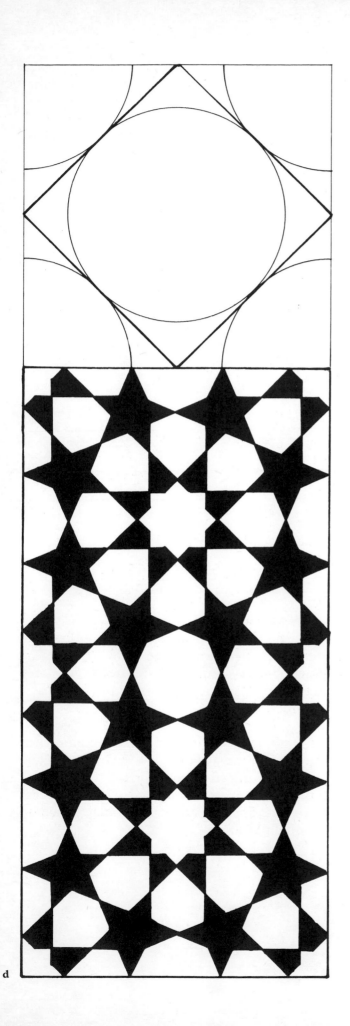

Figures 36a, b, c and d. Figure 36a represents a basic design employed to decorate bands and borders. The square repeat unit in Figure 36a can be bisected by the use of the circle as shown in Figure 36b, and the halves of the repeat pattern can be interchanged to create a new variation of the design. Other variations can also be achieved, and one example is shown in Figures 36c and d where the diagonal of the original square repeat unit is rotated through 45°. The whole (d) or half (c) of the new repeat pattern can be used to generate border designs.

49

3 The Hexagon and the Root Three System of Proportion

The designs presented in this section are based on the master grid of the hexagonal star. The initial procedure for obtaining the size of the repeat unit is the same as described in section 2 of this chapter. Once again one side of the area to be decorated is subdivided by the use of the compasses into a number of parts equal to the number of times the repeat unit is to be incorporated into the design along this side.

The whole area is then further divided by the circles and the adjacent inscribed hexagons are drawn by the point-joining method (Figure 37). The repeat unit is thus a hexagon, the side of which is equal to the radius of the circumscribing circle. The master grid is formed by the hexagonal stars drawn in this hexagon by joining either the alternate corners of the hexagon (Figure 38a) or the alternate midpoints of the sides (Figure 38b).

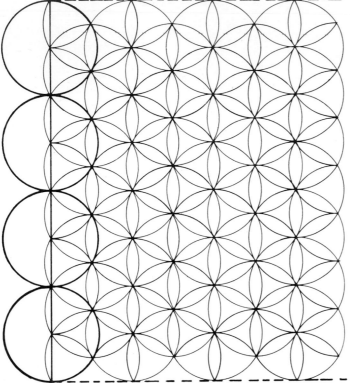

Figure 37a

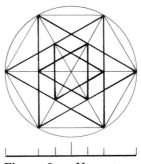
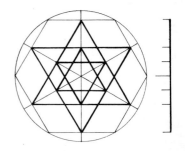

Figure 38a and b

The hexagonal star system (Figure 38a) provides a method of progressively dividing the diameter of the hexagon in the ratio of 1:2. The hexagonal star system (Figure 38b) similarly divides the height of the hexagon in the same ratio of 1:2. Since the ratio of the height AB of the hexagon (Figure 39b), i.e., the side AB of the hexagonal star (Figure 39a), to BC the diameter of the hexagon (Figure 39a or c) is √3:2 a geometric system of relating the two dimensions of the hexagonal repeat unit is achieved without necessitating the use of an arithmetical system based on the irrational numbers.

Figure 37b

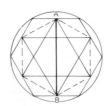
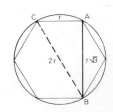

Figure 39a, b and c

Hexagonal tiles, representing the hexagonal repeat unit, have been used to cover surfaces (Figure 100, page 144). However, the hexagonal repeat patterns have also been incorporated into rectangular repeat units to generate the same design (Figure 40).

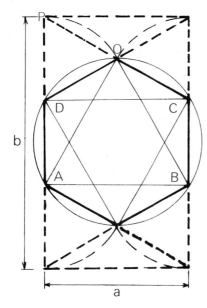

Figure 40

The two sides forming the upper corner O of the hexagonal repeat unit are extended to join the lines through the parallel sides AD and BC of the hexagon. The procedure of extending the two sides forming the lower corner of the hexagon to cut the same parallel sides is repeated, thus forming a rectangle of sides a and b, where a equals the side AB of the hexagonal star and b equals 3r (r is the radius of the circle and the side of the hexagonal repeat unit as indicated), or twice the height of the equilateral triangles forming the hexagonal star; and the triangle AOP is similar to triangle ABC of Figure 39c.

In pages 52 to 81 of this section, geometric designs based on the hexagonal repeat pattern are analysed in the manner explained in the previous section.

Figure 41

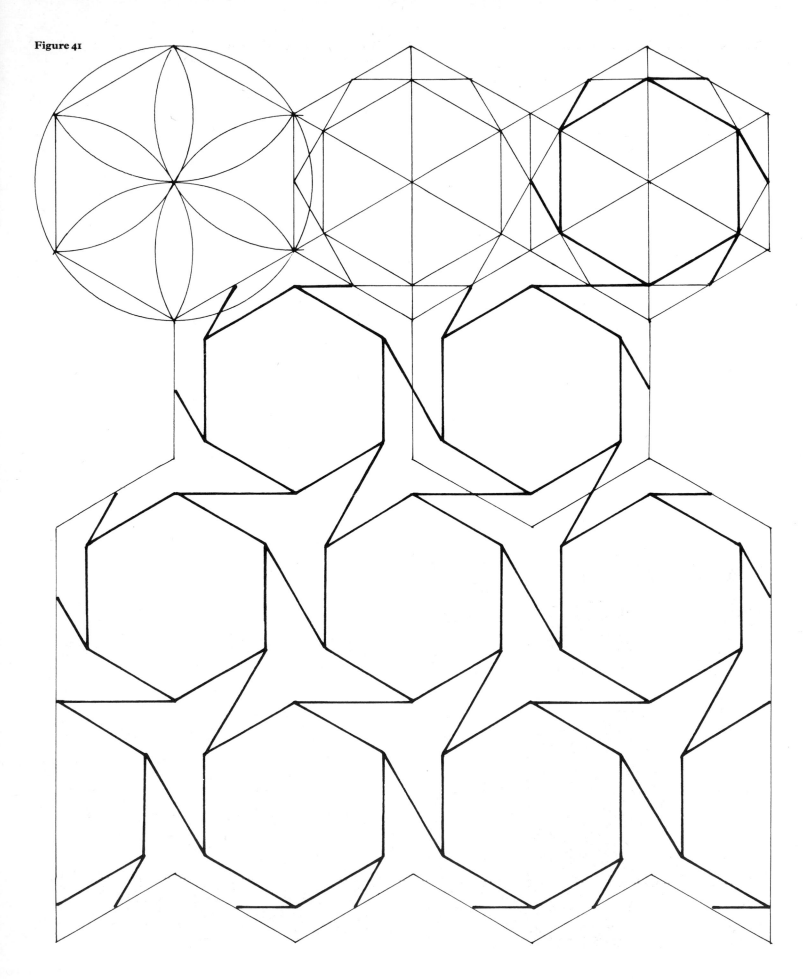

Plate 18. Topkapi Palace, Istanbul, Turkey.

Plate 19. Shibām-Kawkabān, Yemen, late 3rd/9th or early 4th/10th century.

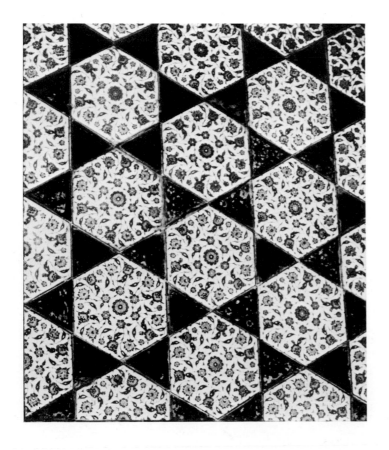

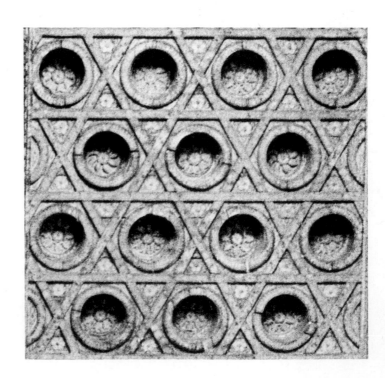

Figure 42

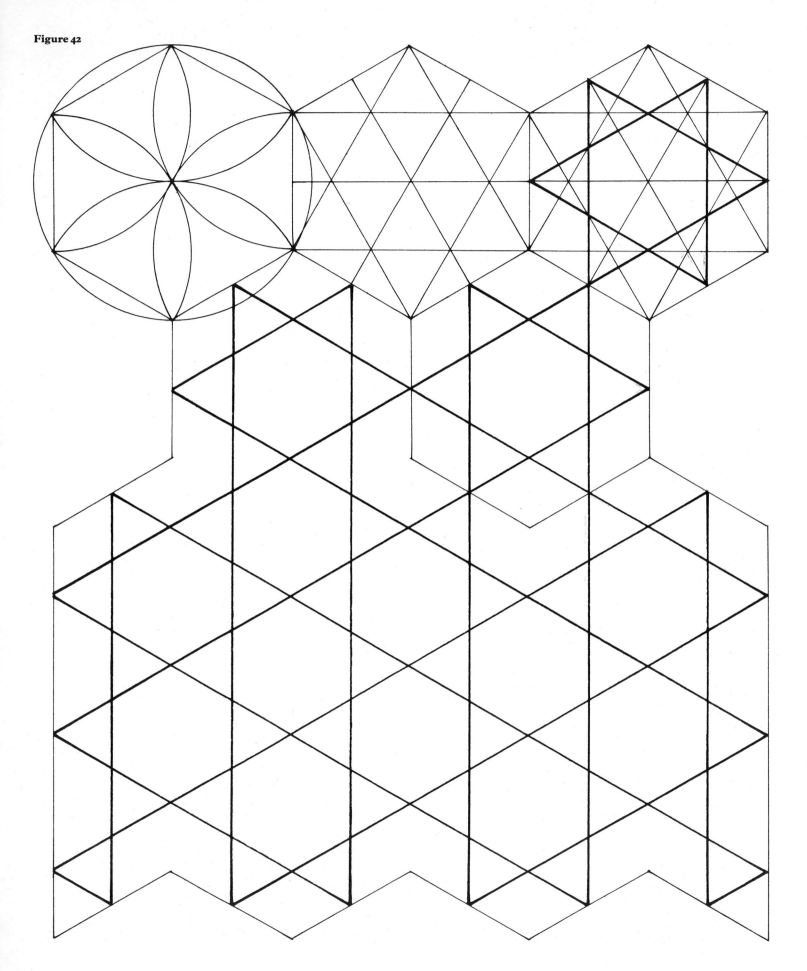

Plate 20. Detail of Persian manuscript, 12th/18th century.

Figure 43

Plate 21. Tomb towers, Kharraqān, Iran, 459/1067.

Figure 44

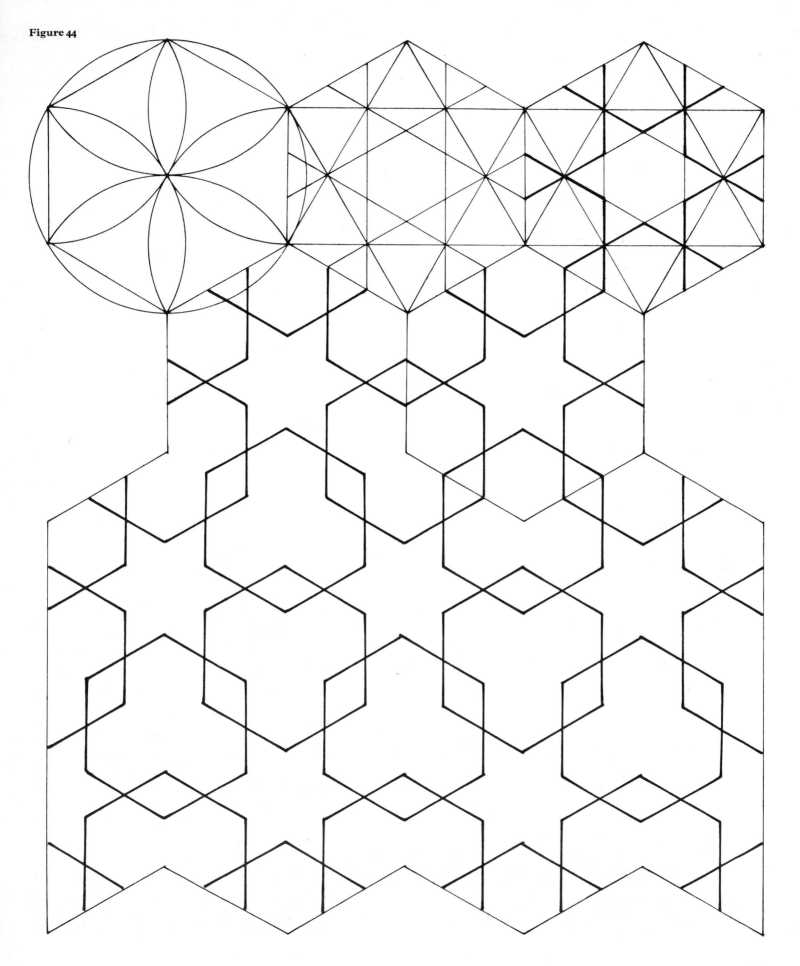

Plate 22. Tomb of Akbar, Sikandra, India, 1021/1612–3.

Figure 45

Plate 23. Tomb towers, Kharraqān, Iran, 459/1067.

Figure 46

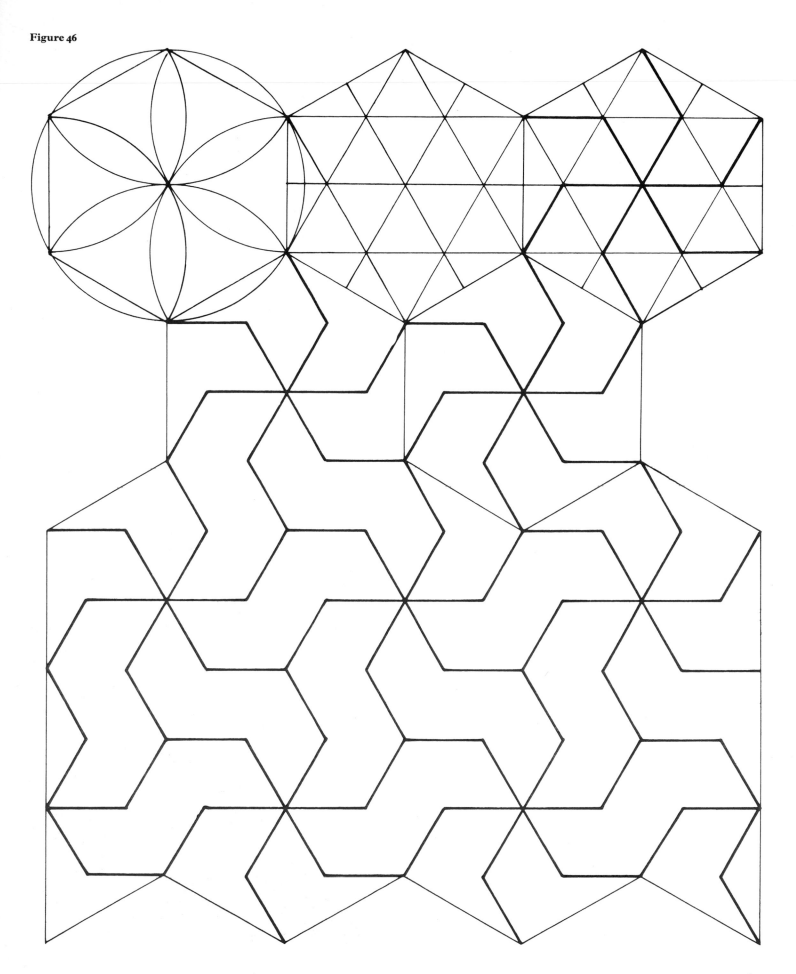

Plate 24. Tomb towers, Kharraqān, Iran, 459/1067.

Figure 47

Plate 25. Mustanṣiriyyah Madrasah, Baghdad, Iraq, 620/1223.

Figure 48

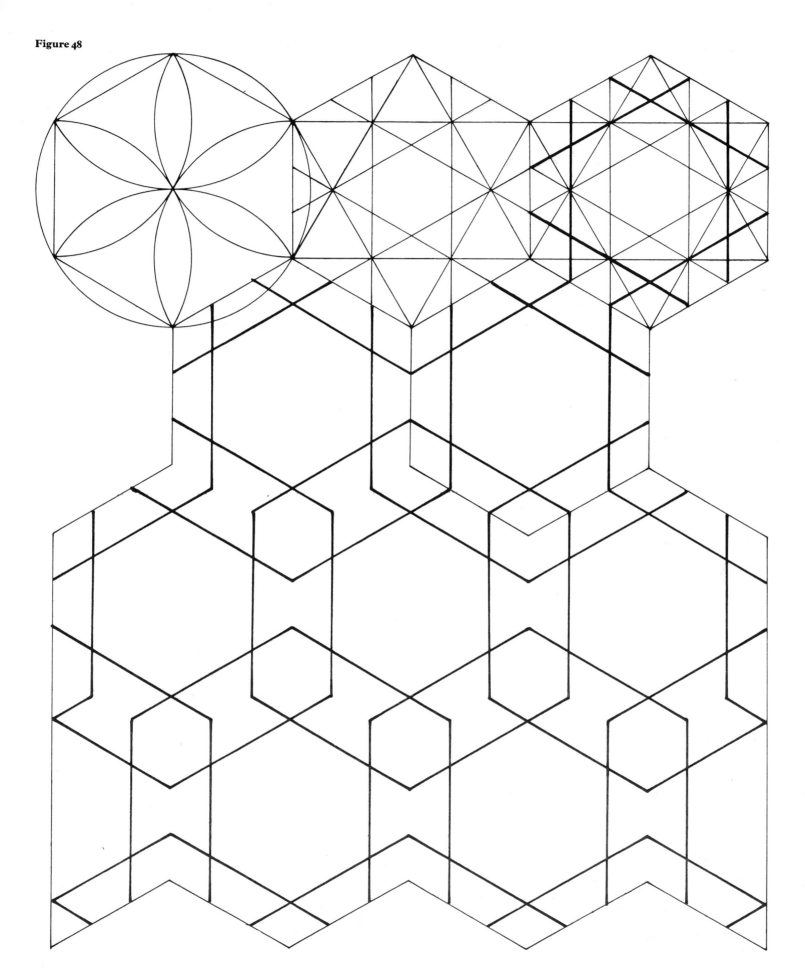

Plate 26. Detail from the *Khamsah* of Niẓāmī, Herat, Afghanistan, 899/1494.

Figure 49

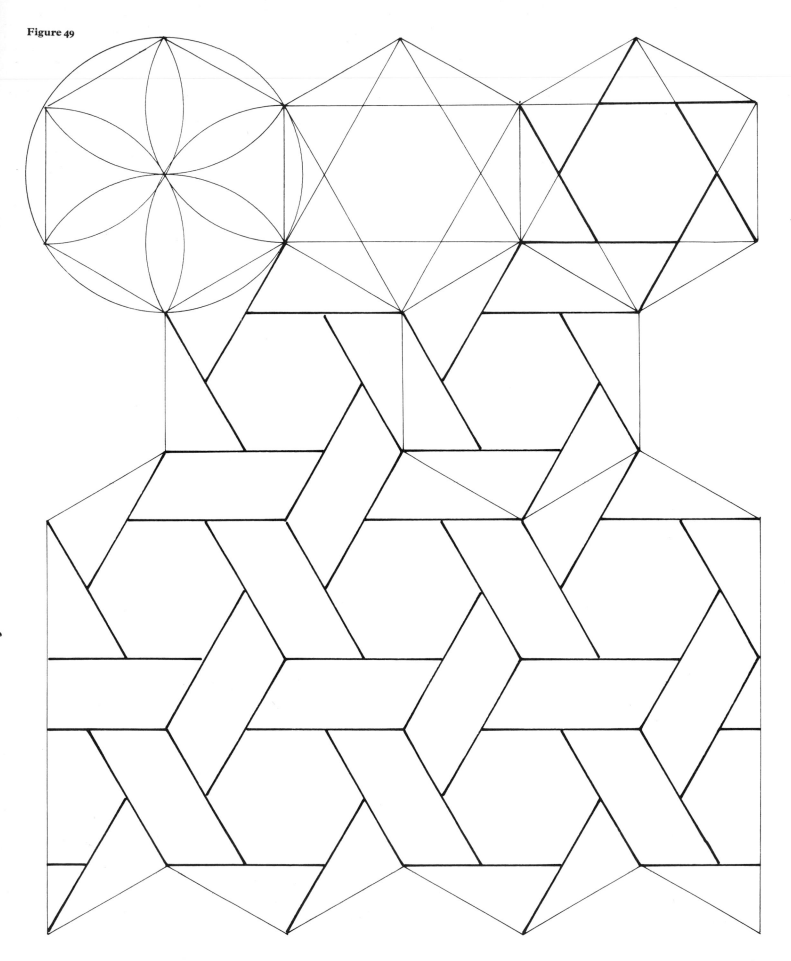

Plate 27. Chehel Dukhtarān, Isfahan, Iran, 5th/11th century.

Figure 50

Plate 28. Tomb towers, Kharraqān, Iran, 459/1067.

Figure 51

Plate 29. Masjid-i-Jāmi, Varzaneh, Iran, mid 9th/15th century.

74

Figure 52

Plate 30. Mustanṣiriyyah Madrasah, Baghdad, Iraq, 620/1223.

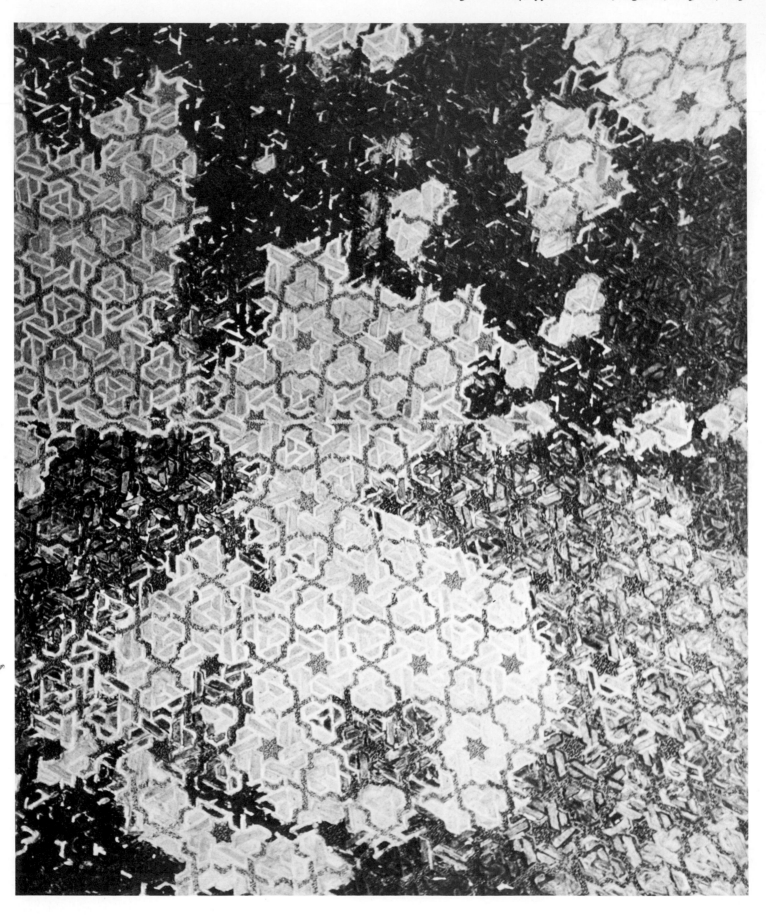

Figure 53

Figure 54

Figure 55

Figure 56

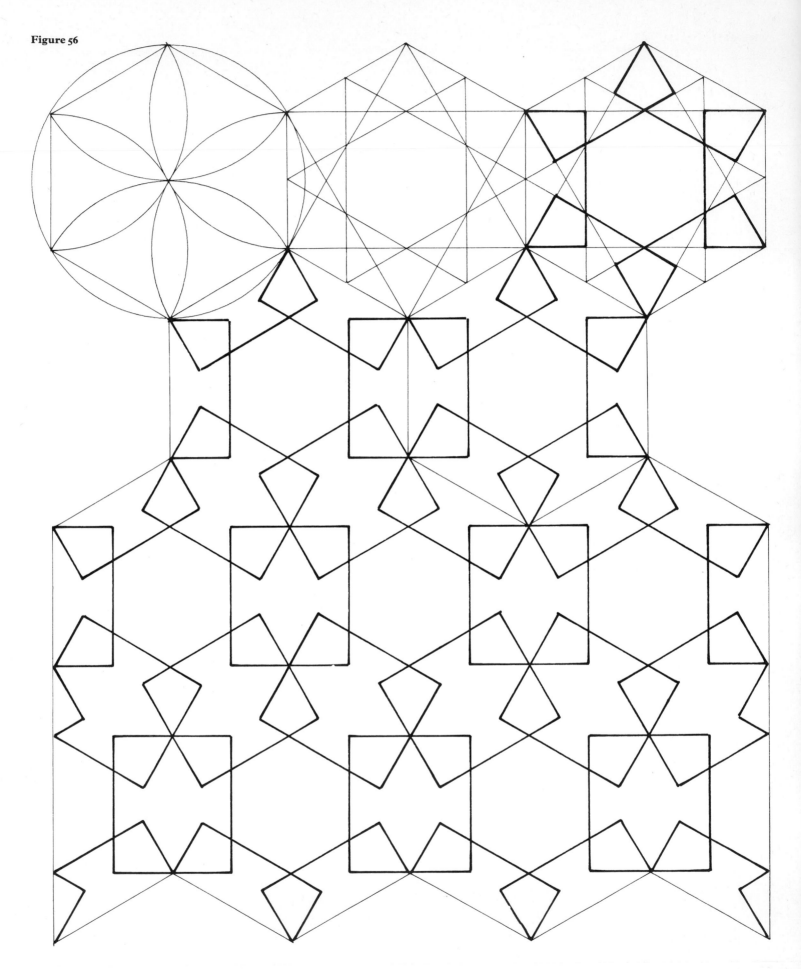

Figure 57

4   The Pentagon and the Golden Ratio

Euclid described the Golden Ratio as the 'extreme and mean ratio'. Renaissance writers referred to it as the 'Divine Proportion', and in the nineteenth century it became known as the 'Golden Section'. At present it is occasionally represented by the letter ϕ, phi, to express the ratio obtained by the following reasoning.

If the ratio between two quantities of the same kind is such that the ratio of the bigger b to the smaller a equals the ratio of the sum of both $a + b$ to the bigger b, that is, $\dfrac{b}{a} = \dfrac{b + a}{b} = \phi$, then we have the Golden Ratio. The Golden Ratio has been represented numerically by the Renaissance scholar, Fibonacci, by means of a series:

$$\frac{b}{a}, \frac{b+a}{b}, \frac{1}{1}, \frac{2}{1}, \frac{3}{2}, \frac{5}{3}, \frac{8}{5}, \frac{13}{8}, \frac{21}{13} \cdots, \phi$$

The series is an approximation which becomes more accurate the higher it goes until it nears the decimal value of ϕ at 1.618.

To divide a straight line AC into two segments related by the Golden Ratio

Given a line AC (Figure 58), draw the perpendicular $DC = \frac{1}{2} AC$, and with D as centre and DC as the radius describe an arc cutting AD at X. With A as centre and AX as the radius describe an arc cutting AC at B.

Then, $\dfrac{AC}{AB} = \dfrac{AB}{BC} = \phi$

To obtain the Golden Ratio from a square

The Golden Ratio ϕ can also be obtained by the use of a square. Bisect at O the side AB of the square ABDE (Figure 59).

Draw diagonal OD, and with centre O and radius OD cut extended AB at C. If $BD = 1$, $OB = \frac{1}{2}$ and, therefore, using the theorem of Pythagoras,

$$OD = OC = \frac{\sqrt{5}}{2}$$

Since $AC = AO + OC$, then:

$$AC : AB = \frac{1}{2} + \frac{\sqrt{5}}{2} : 1 = \phi$$

$$\text{or } \phi = \frac{1 + \sqrt{5}}{2}$$

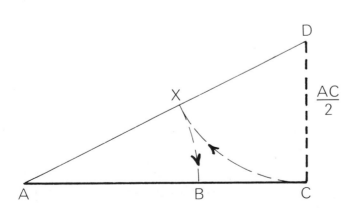

Figure 58

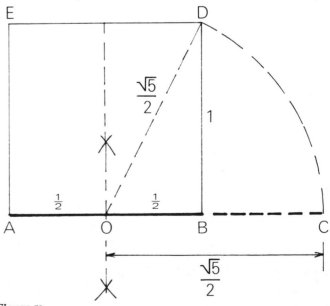

Figure 59

To construct a pentagon with a given side AB

Bisect AB at O (Figure 60), and construct square ABPQ; with O as centre and OP as radius describe a semi-circle intersecting the extensions of AB at C and D. Taking A as centre and AC as radius, describe an arc cutting the perpendicular bisector of AB at X, and with B as centre and BD as radius describe another arc from D intersecting the perpendicular bisector of AB also at X. Then with B as centre and BP as radius describe an arc cutting arc CX at Y, and repeat with A as centre and AQ as radius to cut arc DX at Z. Join points BYXZA to form the regular pentagon.

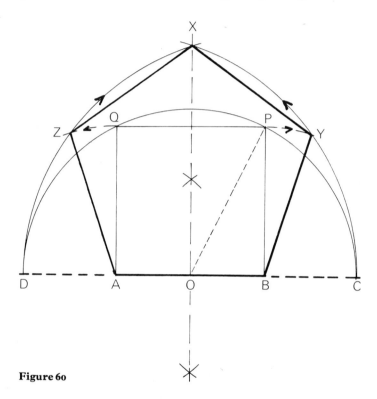

Figure 60

It can be seen that the line AC was obtained by the same procedure as shown in Figure 59, and that AC:AB $= \phi$, i.e., the ratio of the diagonal to the side of the regular pentagon equals the Golden Ratio. The diagonals of the pentagon are the sides of the inscribed pentagonal star (Figure 61a) which cut each other in the proportion ϕ, i.e.

$$\frac{AX}{AG} = \frac{AG}{GX} = \frac{GX}{GH} = \phi, \text{ etc.}$$

The method of constructing a pentagon in a circle has already been given in Figure 4.

In the inscribed decagon Figure 61b, which is derived from the pentagon (as shown earlier in Figure 6), the ratio of the radius OX of the circumscribed circle to the side XE of the decagon and the ratio of the side XF of the star decagon to the radius XO of the circle is equal to the Golden Ratio, i.e., $\dfrac{OX}{XE} = \dfrac{XF}{OX} = \phi$

It can be seen that the regular pentagon and the regular decagon provide the designer with a geometric system of proportioning based on the Golden Ratio.

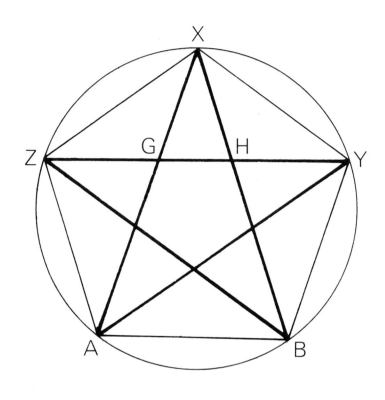

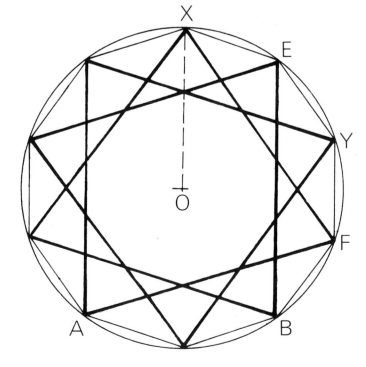

Figures 61a and b

Patterns based on the pentagon and decagon

In this section six patterns are analysed. The master grid of these patterns is the decagonal star. The repeat unit is either a rectangle (Figure 62) or a rhombus (Figure 63) but in the latter case it is easier to use rectangular forms derived from the rhombus.

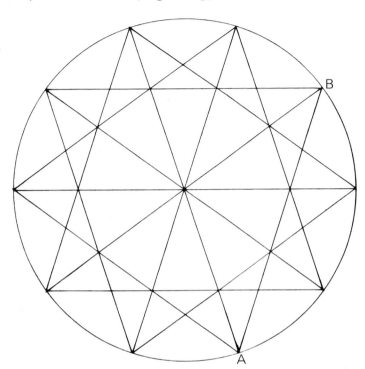

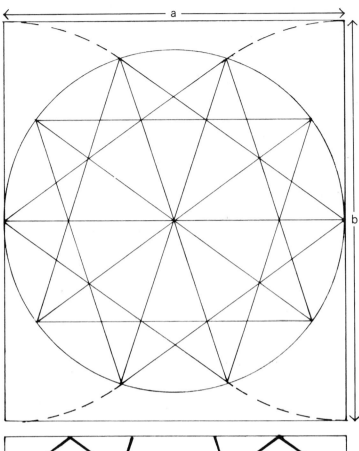

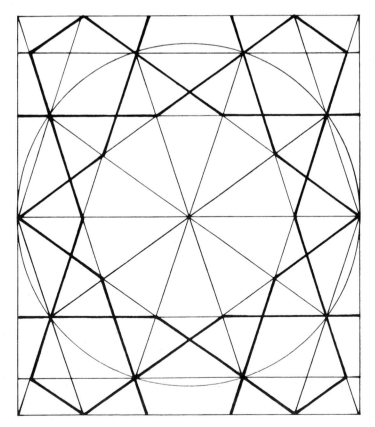

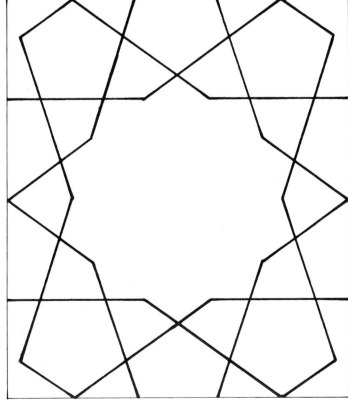

Figure 62a. $a:b = 2r:2AB$ (side of pentagon).

Plate 31. Gazūr Gāh, Herat, Afghanistan, 9th/15th century.

Figures 63a and 63b. a:b = 2 sides of pentagon: 2 sides of star decagon.

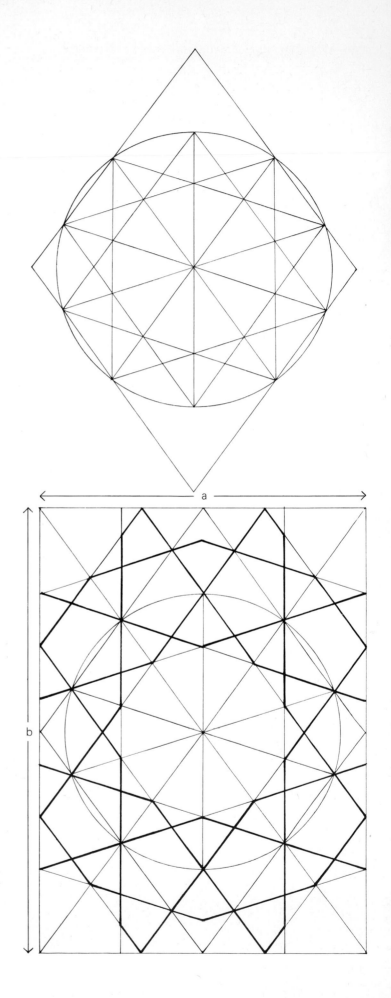

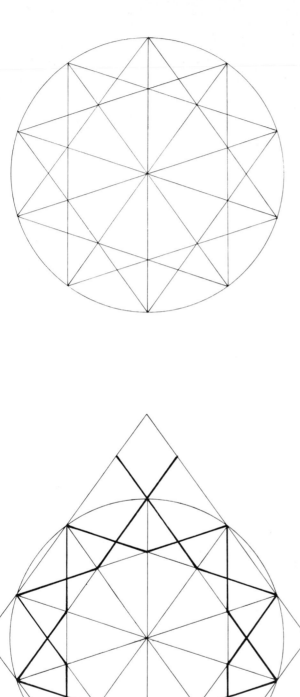

Figure 63a

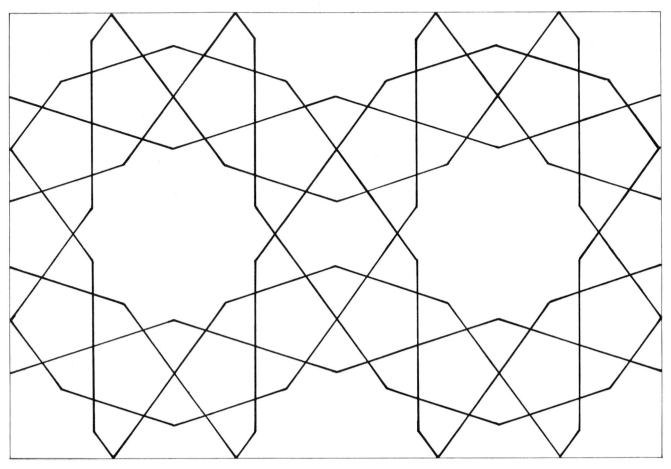

Figure 63b

Plate 32. Mausoleum of I'timād al-Dawla, Agra, India, 1037/1628.

Plate 33. Eighteenth-century tiles from the Masjid-i-Jāmi, Isfahan, Iran.

Figure 64. The repeat pattern of this design is derived similarly to that of the design in Figure 63, but elaborated by the addition of more grid lines within the master grid.

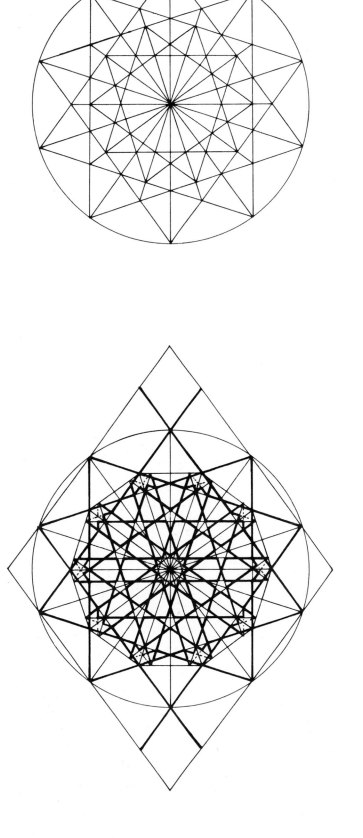
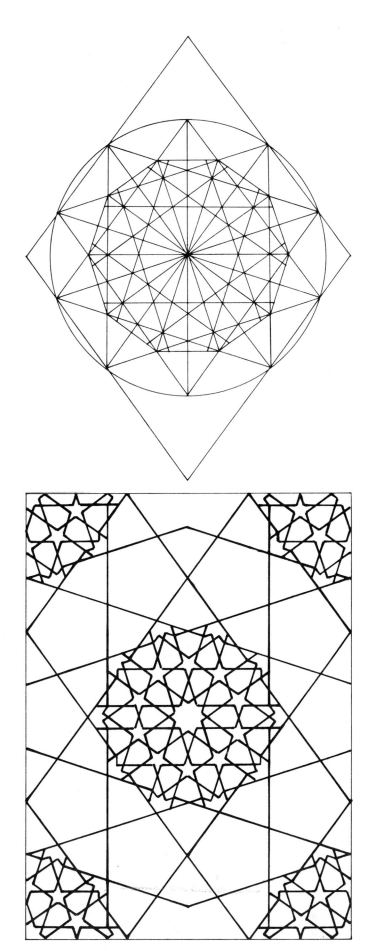

Figure 65a. a : b = 2 sides of pentagon : 2 sides of the star decagon.

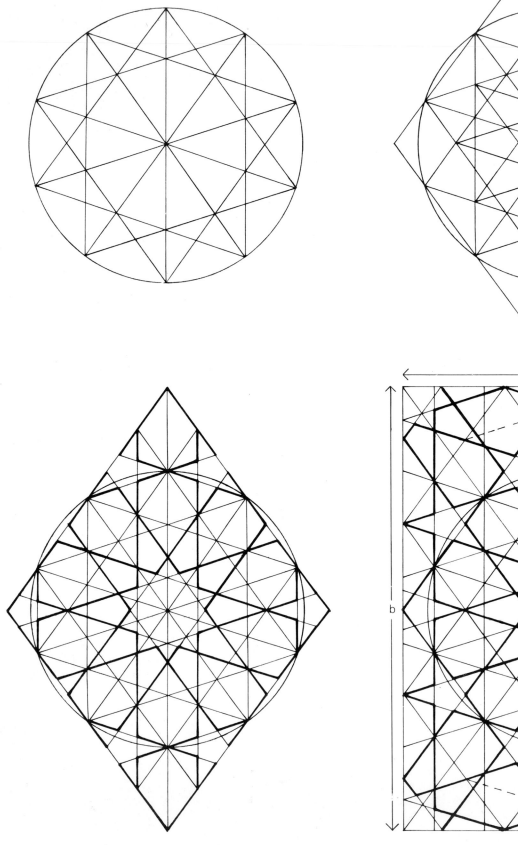
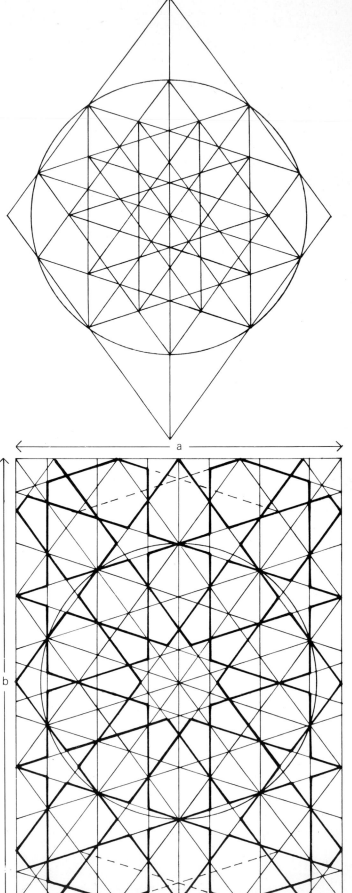

Plate 34. Qal'ah-i-Bist, Afghanistan, late 4th/10th–early 5th/11th century.

Figure 65b

Figure 66a. XW (side of rhombus) = 2 XF (the side of the star decagon).

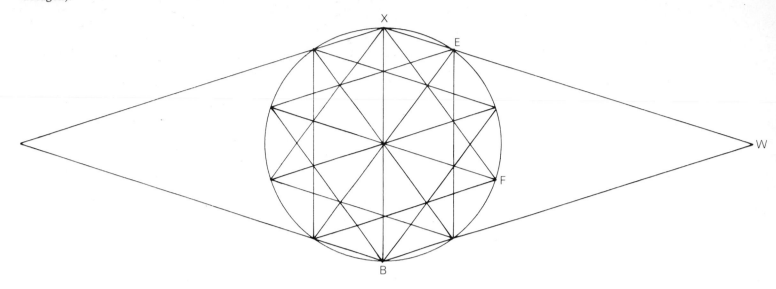

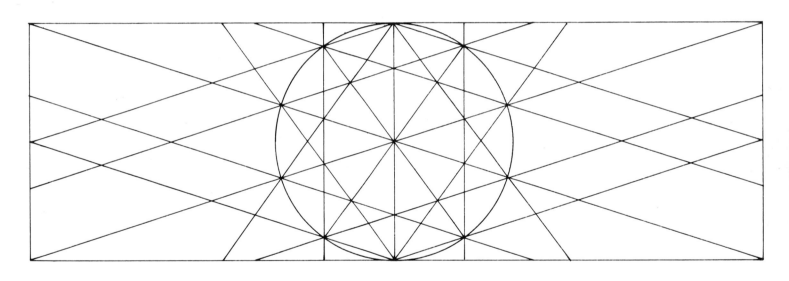

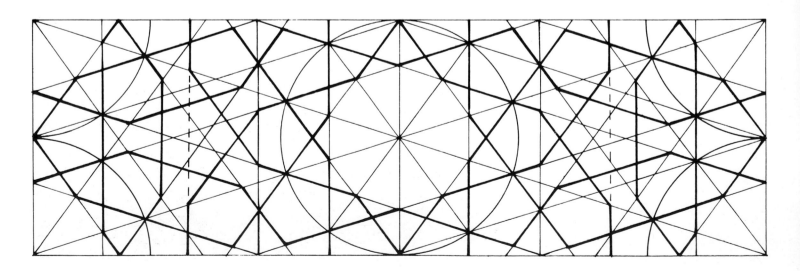

94

Figure 66b

Plate 35. Shrine of Zayn al-Dīn, Ṭayabād, Iran, 9th/15th century.

Figure 67a. XW (side of rhombus) = 2 XF (the side of the star decagon).

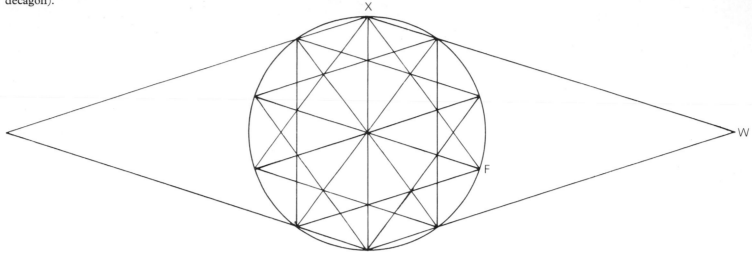

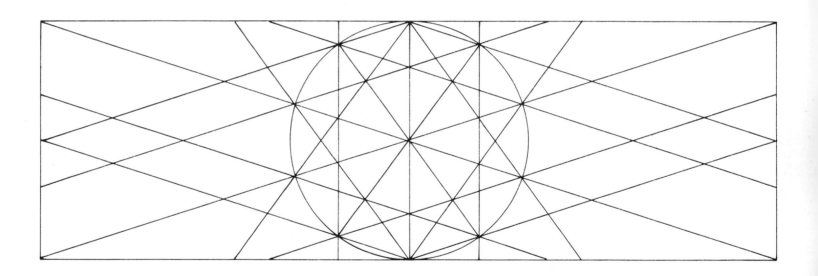

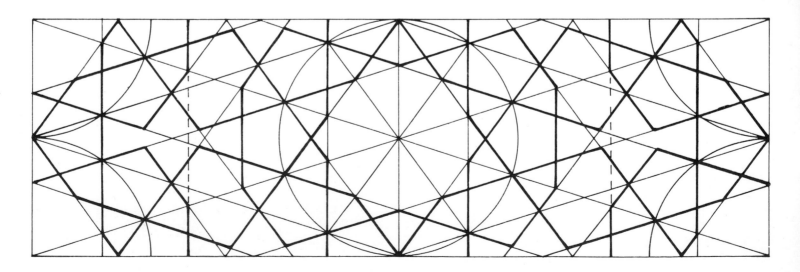

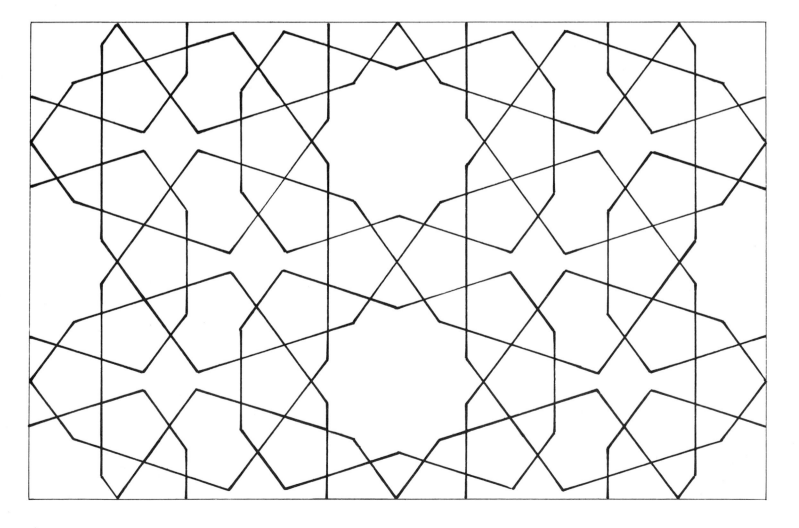

5 Patterns Based on the Double Hexagon

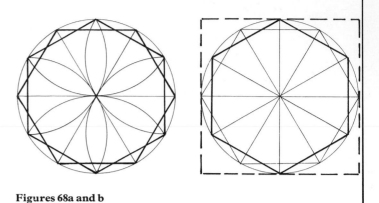

Figures 68a and b

The patterns analysed in this section are generated by dividing the circumference of the circle into twelve equal parts, the process of which has been described earlier in Figure 5b. Two hexagons are inscribed in the circle by joining the alternate points on the circumference (Figure 68).

The repeat unit of the overall design can be one of the inscribed hexagons, or the circumscribed square as shown in Figure 68b, and also in Figures 76, 77 and 78 (pages 106 to 111). The method of equipartitioning the area to be decorated into hexagonal or square repeat units has already been described in sections 1 and 2, respectively, of this chapter. The master grid of the repeat pattern is constructed by inscribing three squares or four equilateral triangles either by using the twelve points of division or the circumference of the circle (Figures 69 and 70 respectively), or by using the midpoints of the sides of the inscribed hexagons (Figures 71 and 72 respectively). Constructing the master grid by the former procedure and generating the grid lines and the repeat patterns of two different designs is also illustrated in detail in Figures 79 and 80.

These particular methods of constructing the master grid established the only system combining the $\sqrt{2}$ and $\sqrt{3}$ system of proportioning (see sections 1 and 2 of this chapter). The resultant repeat patterns thus include equilateral triangles, squares, hexagons, octagons, dodecagons, and their stars, to create the characteristically rich visual harmonies of design illustrated in this section.

Different systems of proportioning can be thus combined when the circumference of the circle is sectioned equally by that number of points on which multiples of the regular polygons providing these particular systems of proportioning can be drawn to give the required master grid. For example, when the circumference is divided into fifteen equal sections, five equilateral triangles or three pentagons can be inscribed to give the master grid which combines the proportioning systems based on the $\sqrt{3}$ and the Golden Section. The resultant repeat patterns would be characterized by triangles, pentagons and their multiples combined with their respective stars.

Plate 36. Tomb towers, Kharraqān, Iran, 459/1067.

Figure 69

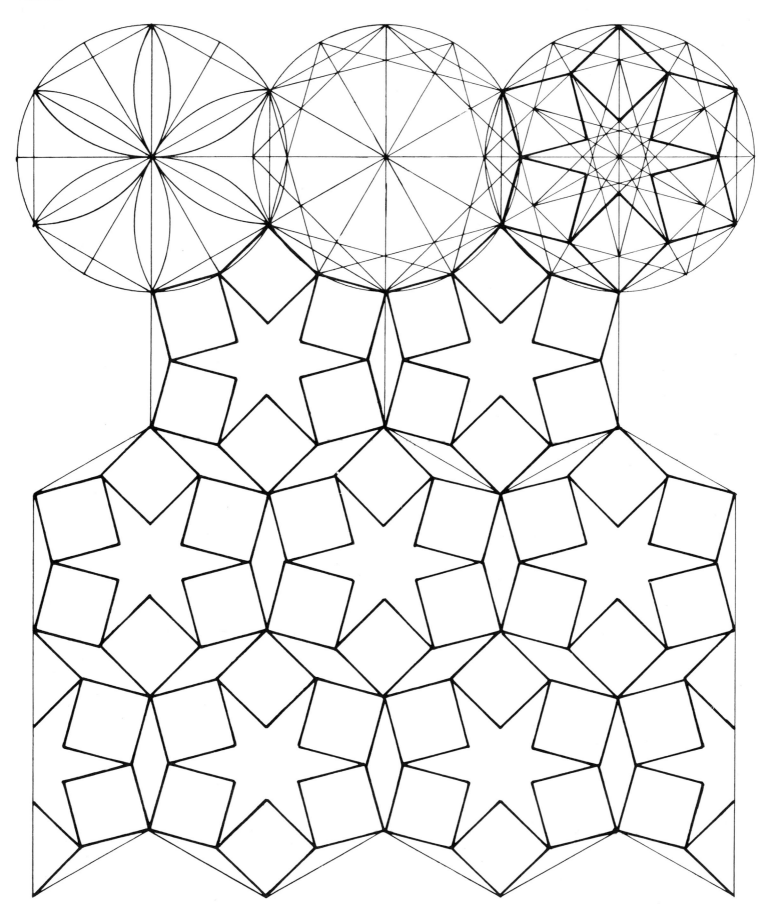

Figure 70

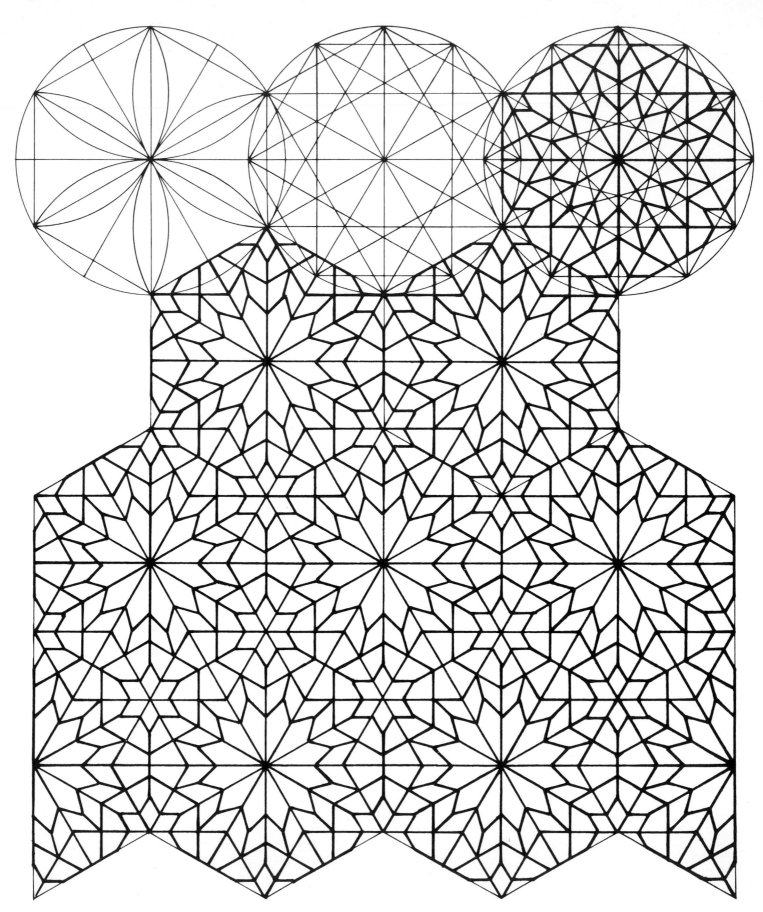

Plate 37. Shibām-Kawkabān, Yemen, late 3rd/9th or early 4th/
10th century.

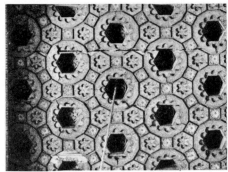

Figure 71

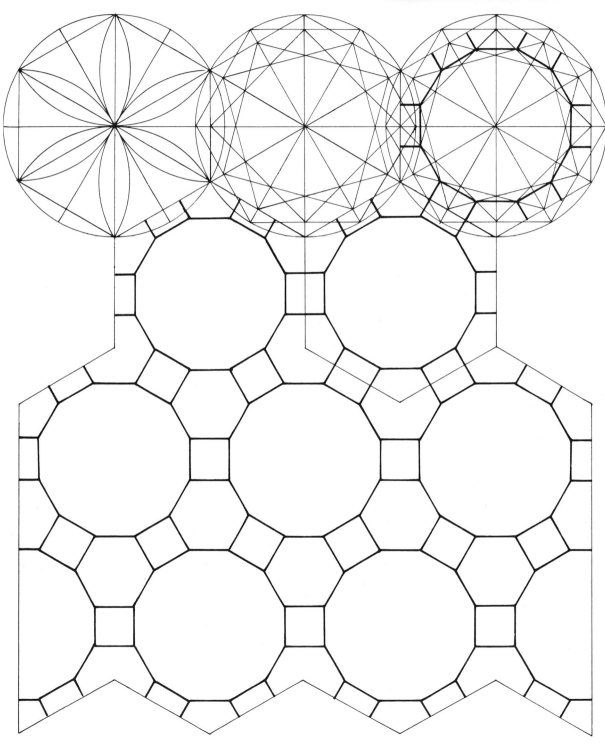

Figure 72

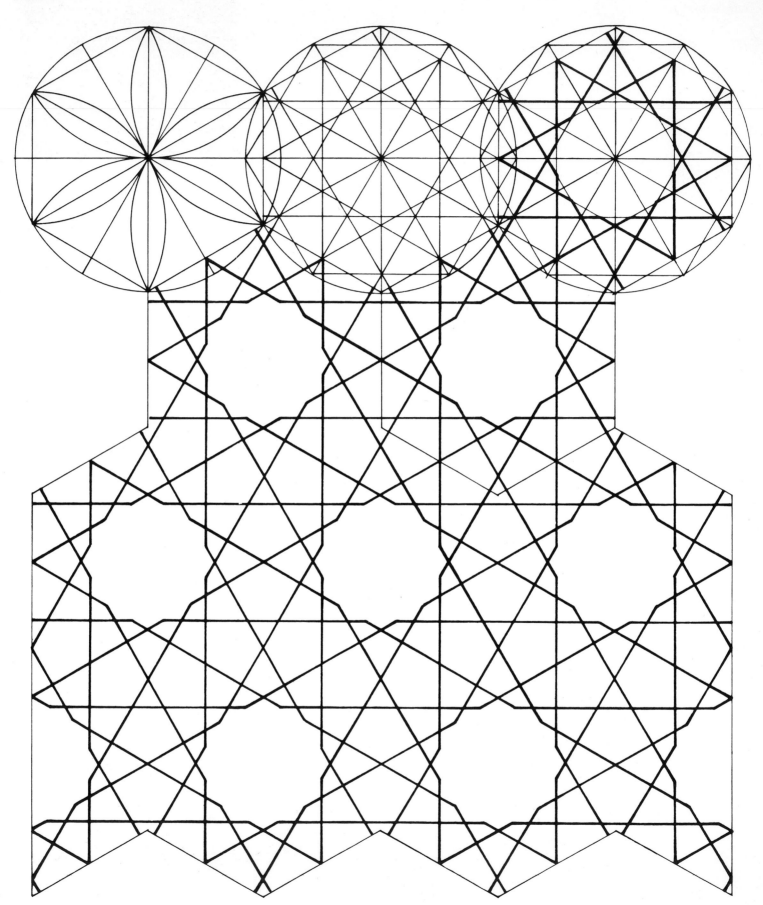

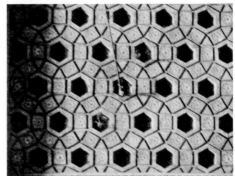

Figure 73

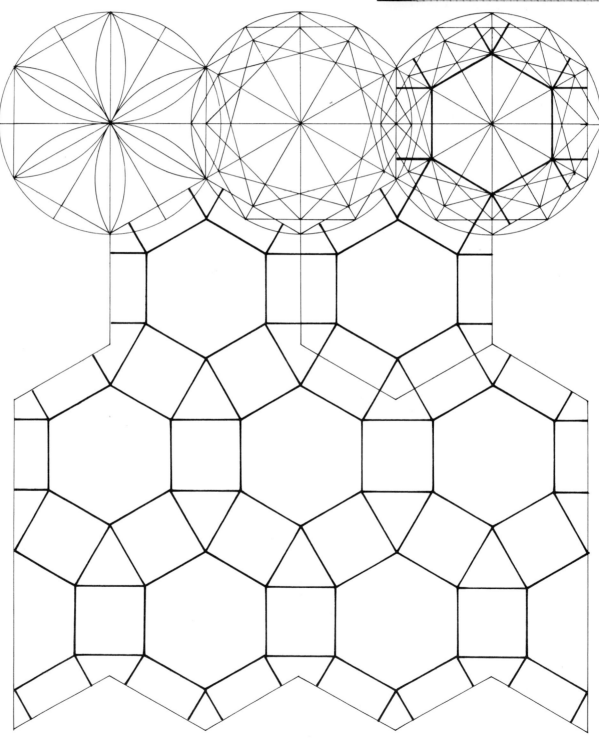

Figure 74

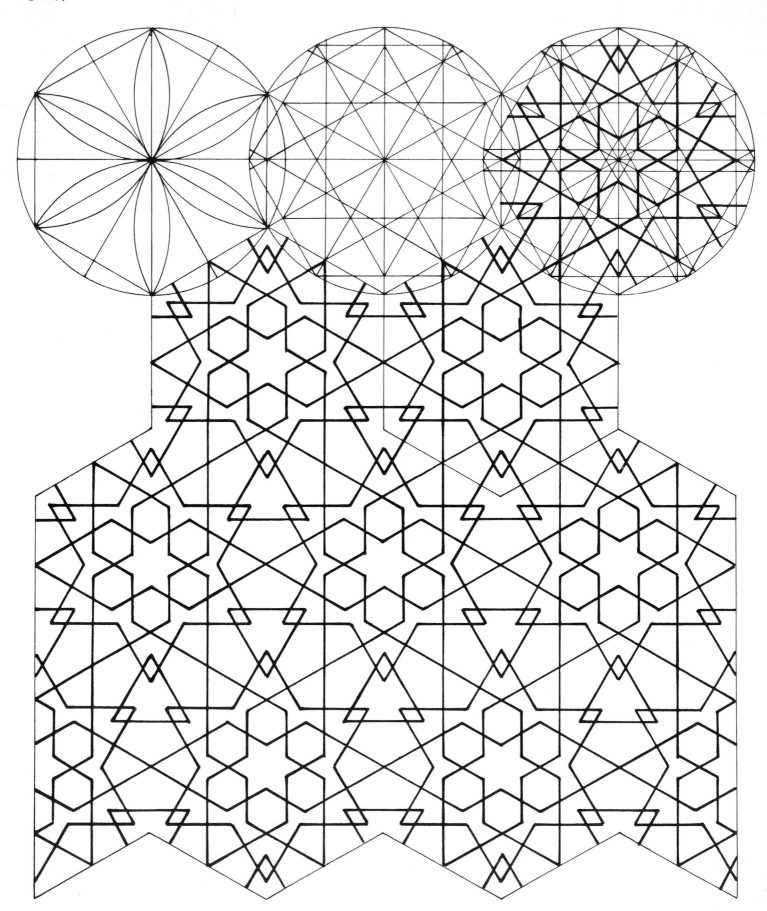

Figure 75

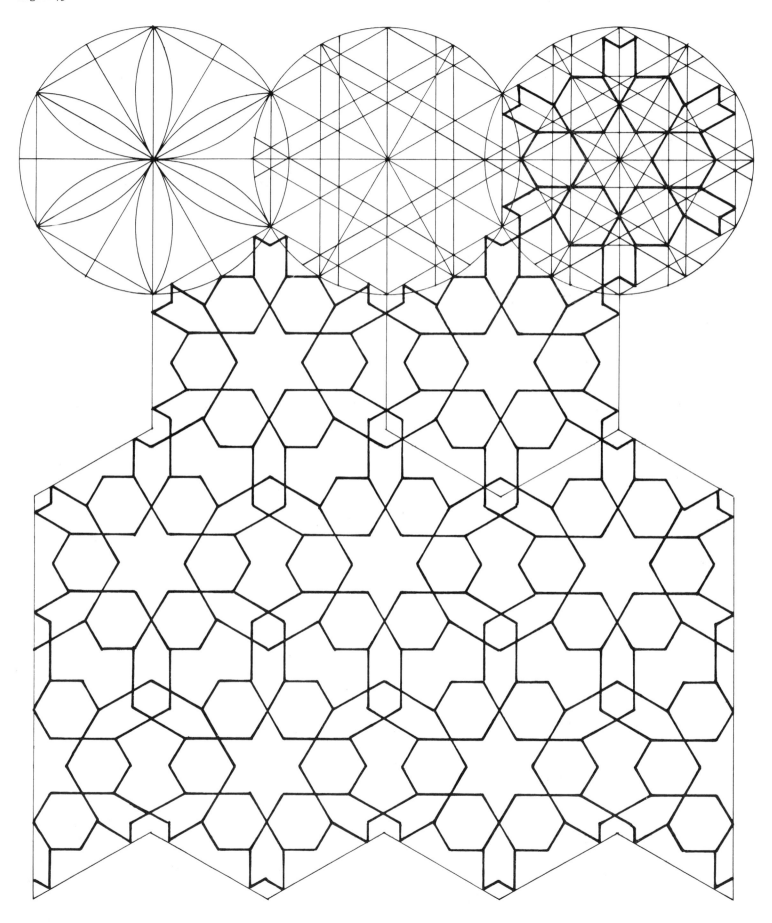

Plate 39. Dome of the Rock, Jerusalem.

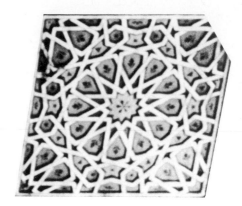

Figure 76a

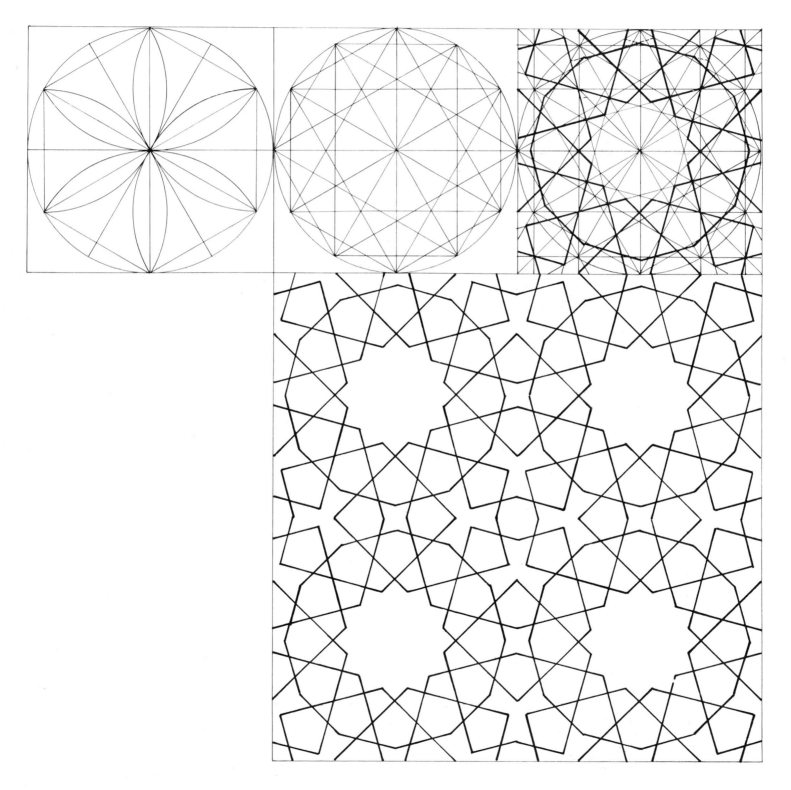

Plate 40. Dome of the Rock, Jerusalem.

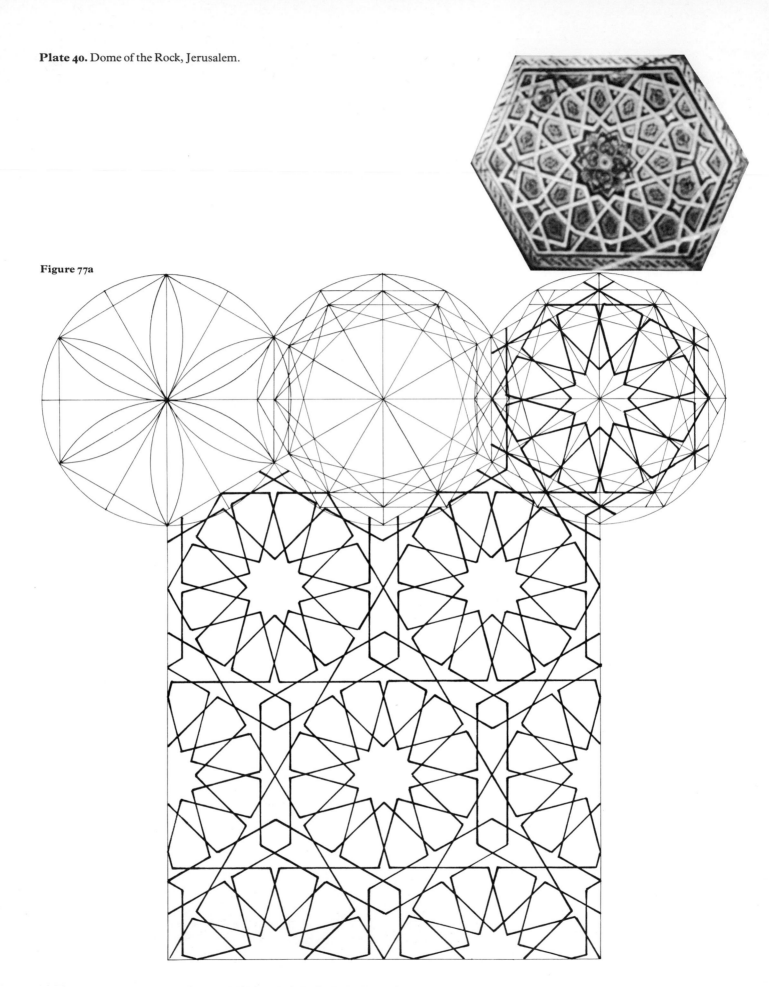

Figure 77a

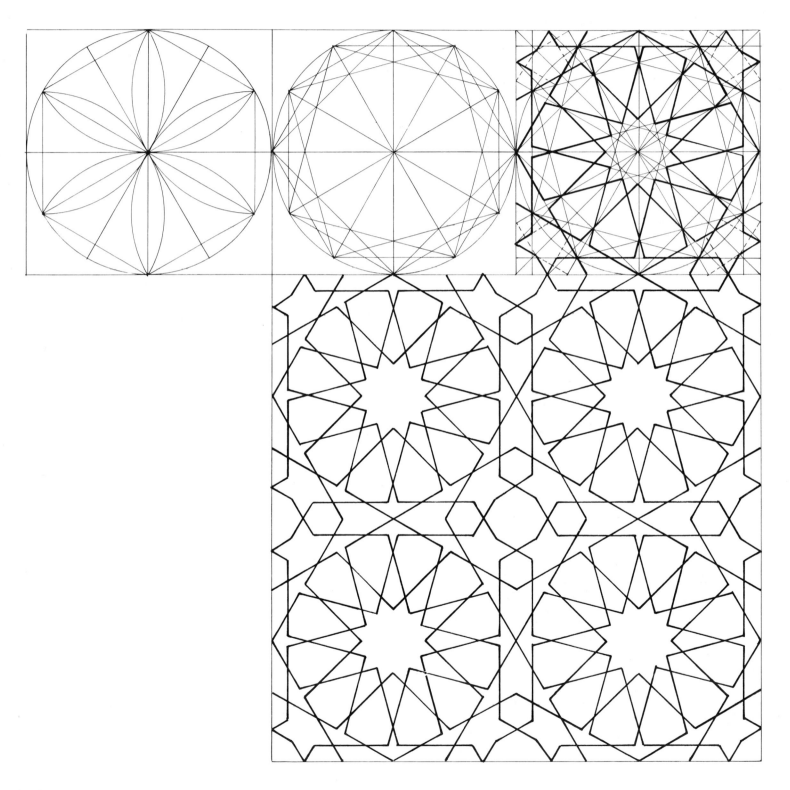

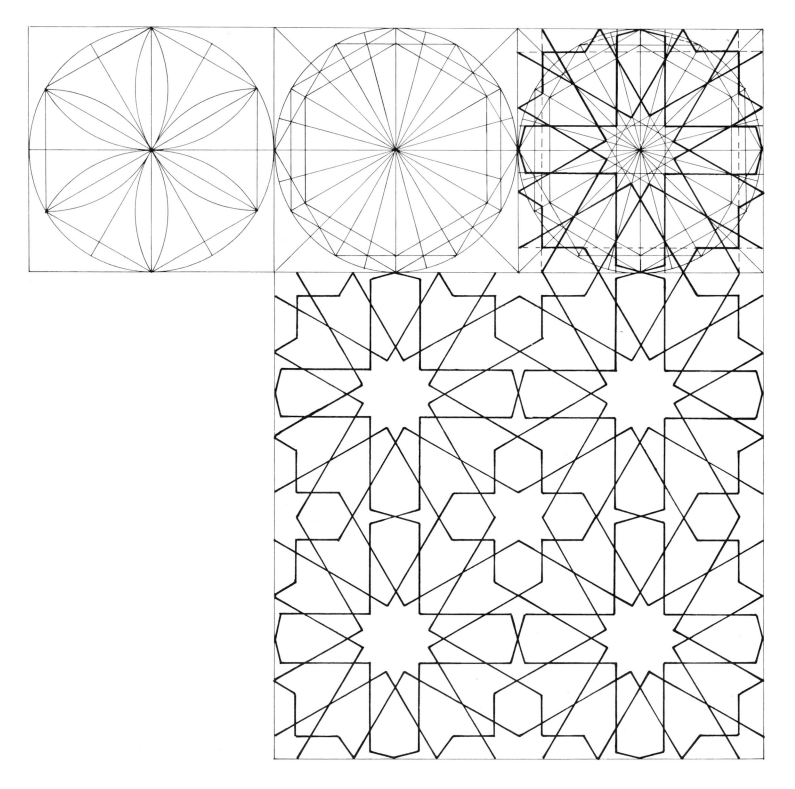

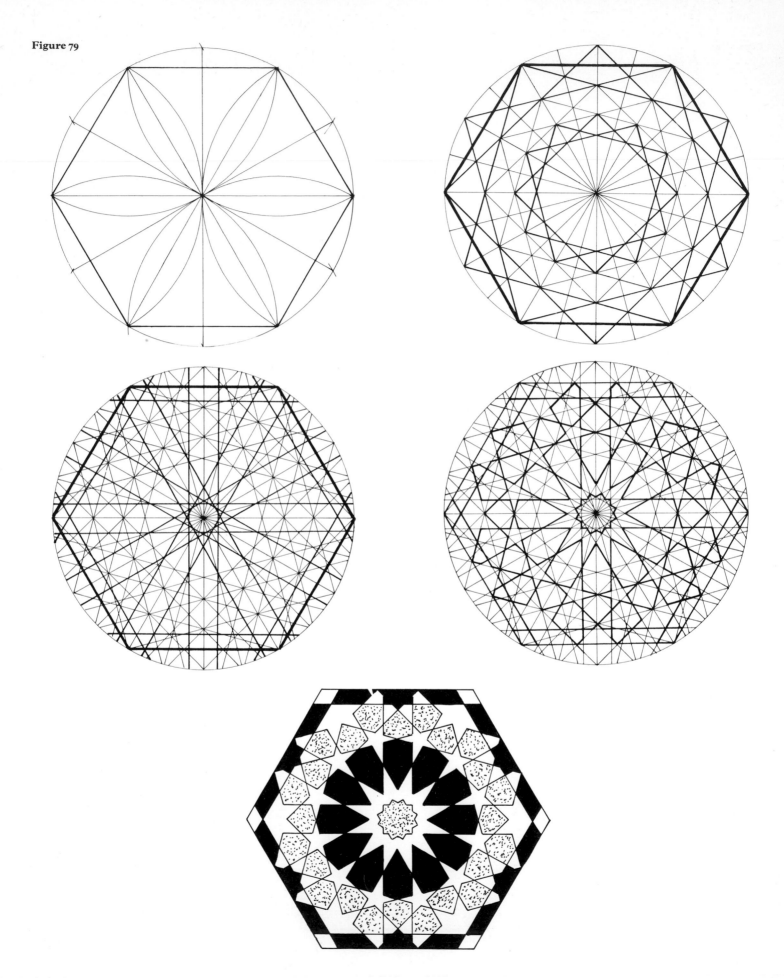

Figure 79

Figure 80

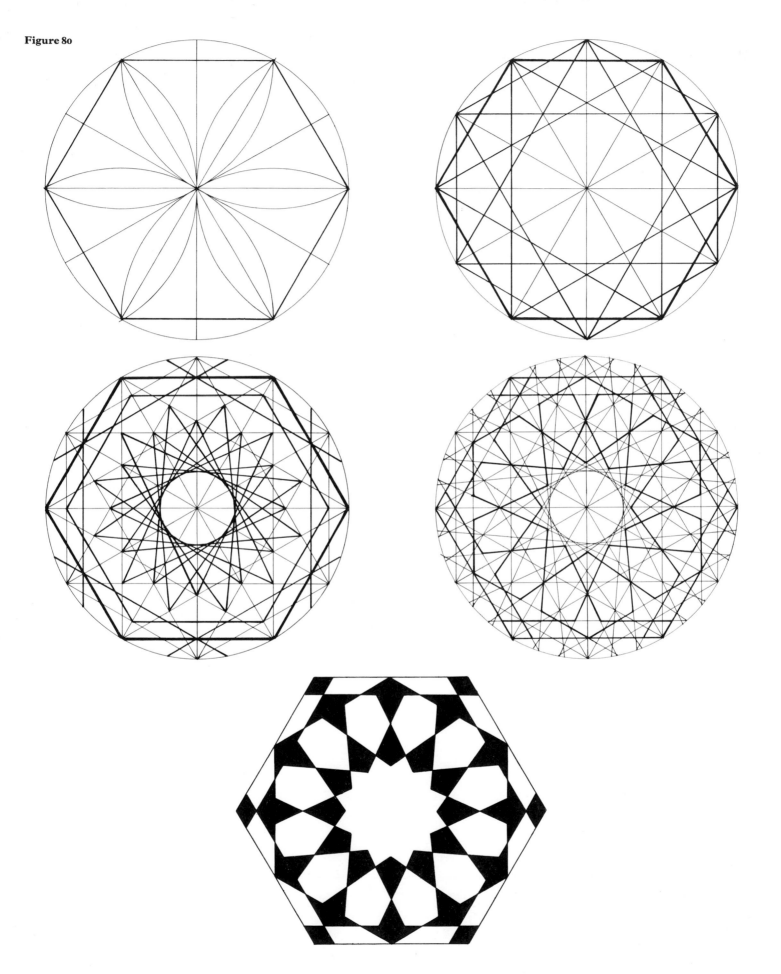

6 Artistic Creativity and the Geometric Method of Design

Geometric patterns are constructed by the recurrence of geometrical forms, the resultant ordering of which is determined by the creative act. When the systems of proportioning have been selected, the creation of patterns by infinite combinations of the geometric forms providing these systems of proportioning becomes possible. The designer thus has the freedom of choosing his systems of construction as well as the freedom of constituting the variations made possible by these systems. The geometric method therefore establishes an approach to art in which the execution and the aesthetics of the composition is systematically determined. However, it cannot be regarded as a purely mechanical process on account of its capacity to accommodate human self-expression. The reader must now conceive that the ability to exploit the freedom of expression by the geometric method necessitated a deep familiarity with the available systems of construction only acquired after long periods of experience. The knowledge gained in this field, being very broad and detailed, was only transmitted through apprenticeship. The artistic achievement, as in music, was an abstract or intellectual beauty arising from order or 'truth', with expressiveness and originality based on the depth of knowledge and skill, in that order, the joyful pursuit of the usually 'anonymous' artist who thus wove his identity into his work.

References

1. Bourgoin, J. and Hankin, E. H.

Chapter III
Architecture

Architecture, the craft of building, involves definite planning to attain unity of form. The transition from primitive building to architecture must have been attained by the introduction of mensuration. The earliest constructions we know to have been accurately planned are the Sumerian temples of the fourth millennium B.C. Although the need for shelter first motivated man to start building, architecture, as defined here, also had the spiritual function of 'sheltering' the gods and the dead. The main significance of the temples and pyramids lay in their external forms and ensured visual recognition of their architectural construction as monuments. It was geometry, the language of architecture, which made possible the diverse stylistic developments for exteriors not only to indicate a function but also, as in other art forms, to evoke an emotional response. This was achieved by the organization of the constructional and decorative elements, e.g., columns, arches, and windows, in definite proportion to the dimensions of the complete structure. For example, the Doric, Ionic and Corinthian Greek orders were distinguished by the relative proportions of their constituent constructional and decorative elements and were used to express ideas and feelings of grandeur, solemnity or joy – the very reasons for describing architecture as 'frozen music'.

I Tracing Islamic Methods to a Possible Origin

Architectural planning is basically geometrical organization of areas. In the previous chapter we demonstrated how it would be possible to organize small areas (i.e., a repeat unit and the repeat pattern of a design) by the use of compasses and rule. When considering work on the architectural scale, however, an implement or a method replacing the compasses has to be thought of. The earliest possible method we could refer to is that of the rope-stretchers (temple surveyors) in ancient Egypt.[1] Since not much has come to be known of the techniques of the rope-stretchers, one has to attempt to deduce the simplest possible methods employed from the relevant historical evidence so far made available.

Ropes with twelve equidistant knots have been found in Egypt. A reel of these knotted ropes was included in the pictorial representation of Sesheta (also known as Sefkhet meaning 'seven' and distinguished by seven plumettes on her head) who was the goddess of construction, 'the lady of the builder's measure',[2] 'the founder of architecture'.[3] Planning in the field was referred to as spreading or unfurling the plan net,[4] which appeared to be a reference to establishing 'grid lines' on the building site. Foundation ceremonies,[5] when the net was spread, took place on favourable days appointed by the Pharaoh who also insured that the planning was conceived in the traditional 'divine order'[6] and participated in its application.[7] He has been pictured placing down the peg while the rope-stretchers with the rope attached to this peg began the planning, e.g., tracing a circle around the peg as a centre or marking distances in knots along a straight line.

The Ancient Egyptians employed a duo-decimal system of mensuration.[8] The short cubit (approximately 49.9 cm) consisted of two feet, six palms or twenty-four digits (each equivalent to the breadth of one finger). This system together with the Assyrian mensuration system involving a cubit of approximately 54.9 ± 0.5 cm formed the basis of the Greek and Roman mensuration systems. Ancient Egyptian mathematics employed the fraction as a means of progressively doubling or halving as well as of adding and computing differences.[9] For planning, their geometric system has been shown to incorporate the square (e.g., square grids), the triangle (the $3:4:5$ right-angled triangle) and the $1:2$, $1:4$, and $1:8$, and $8:5$ (height:base) isosceles triangles.[10]

Using this information a geometric analysis of three Egyptian monuments has been presented below. The aim of these analyses is to demonstrate that these plans, unlike the hitherto presented arbitrary point-joining analyses, were constructed by a reproducible geometric method based on the circle, and its inscribed and circumscribed polygons, the diameters, the radii and the diagonals respectively, forming the key grid lines which related perfectly to the outlines of the plan of the building.

The geometrical basis of the analysis

(i) Division of the circumference of the circle into twenty-four equal segments is achieved either by constructing a square (Figure 81a) and by joining points of the intersecting arcs by straight lines through the centre of the circle (Figure 3) or by using the inscribed double hexagon in Figure 81b (see also the illustrations and the text on pages 4 and 98).

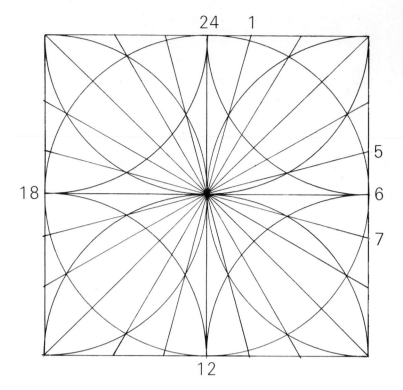

Figure 81a

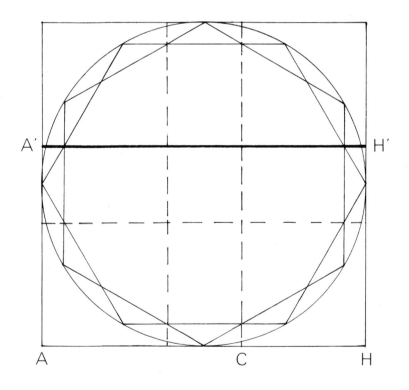

Figure 81b

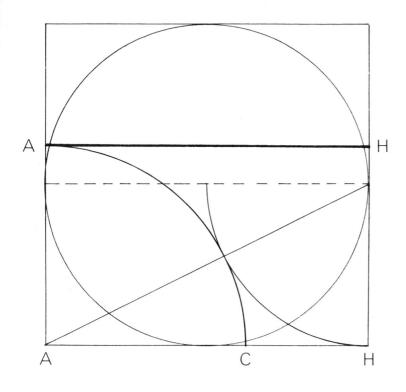

A

H

A   C   H

Figure 81c

(ii) The contemporary method of constructing a 'golden rectangle' within a square is given in Figure 81c (see also Figure 59 and text). The golden rectangle, indicated by the heavy lines in Figures 81b and c, is so named because the ratio of its length to its width is equal to ϕ, i.e., the 'Golden Ratio'. The width of the golden rectangle can be seen from Figure 81a to be equal to the linear distance between points 24 and 5 or points 7 and 12 on the circumscribed square, which is also the distance A'A or H'H in Figures 81b and c.

(iii) A straight line AH, where HB = AC, can be progressively subdivided in the proportion $\phi = \dfrac{AB}{BC} = \dfrac{BC}{CD} = \dfrac{CD}{DE}$ etc., as shown in Figures 82a. The application of this method of subdivision to the side AH of the circumscribed square in Figure 82b and joining the points of intersection (e.g., B', C') of the sides of the golden rectangles with the diagonals would give a series of rectangles (indicated by heavy lines) the sides of which are related to the same proportions of approximately ϕ. It can be seen in Figure 82c that this method also gives the series of squares the sides of which are related in the proportion of ϕ. These squares, e.g., A'C'AC, C'H'C''H'', D''H''DH, etc., are also referred to as the 'whirling squares'.

(iv) As we have already said in Chapter I, the use of linear numerical measure in geometric or architectural designing would involve irrational numbers with which civilizations before the eighth century A.D. could not deal. The square (or second power) of irrational numbers being rational numbers, a linear progression of square areas can be obtained by the use of dynamic rectangles within ACYX (see also Figure 10) as shown in Figure 82d, where the diagonal of the fourth dynamic rectangle whose long side is equal to $\sqrt{5}$ sections side AH at C in the proportion

$$\frac{AC}{CH} = \frac{AH}{AC} = \phi.$$

This method provides a scale to be used for proportioning in the construction or the analysis of the outlines of architectural plans, as applied in the second and third analysis of Egyptian monuments given below.

Figure 82

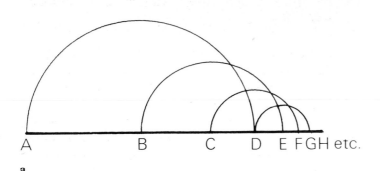

a

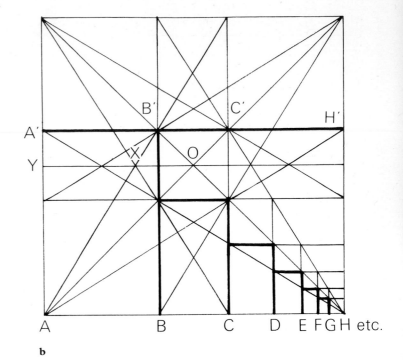

b

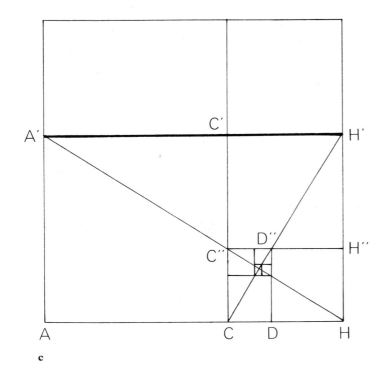

c

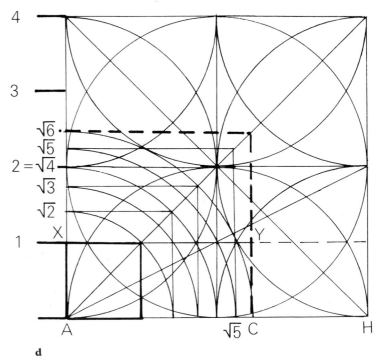

d

2 Analyses of Ancient Egyptian Monuments

(a) Temple of Sesostris I at Tod (XIIth dynasty, c. 1950 B.C.)[11]

The Temple (Figure 83b), excluding the thickness of the walls along the length, is a 2:3 rectangle, consisting (in this analysis) of 24 unit squares. Following the explanation given to (Figure 82d) the three scale dimensions used in this plan (Figure 83a) are the diagonal ($= \sqrt{2}$ units) of the unit square, the diagonal ($= \sqrt{5}$ units) of the double unit square (or the 1:2 rectangle which is known to have assumed great importance in the outline of plans and façades in Ancient Egypt)[12] and the hypotenuse ($= 2.5$ units of the $\frac{3}{2}:\frac{4}{2}:\frac{5}{2}$ right-angled triangle) of the Osiris triangle;[13] these are indicated by the dotted lines in Figure 83a.

Figures 83a, b and c

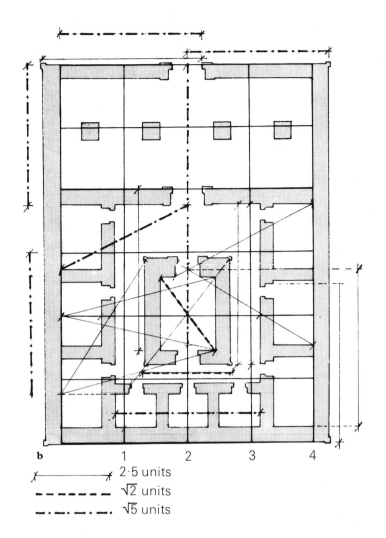

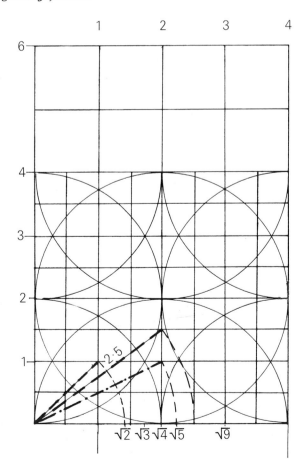

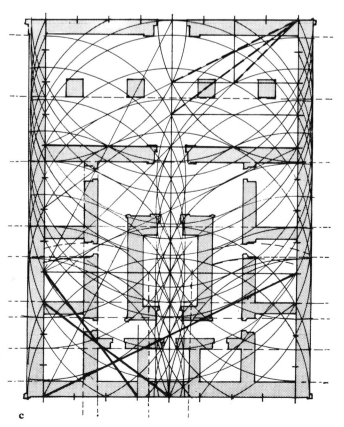

Figure 84a

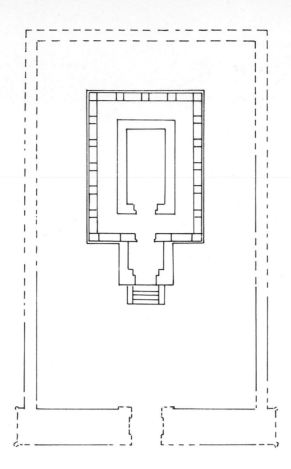

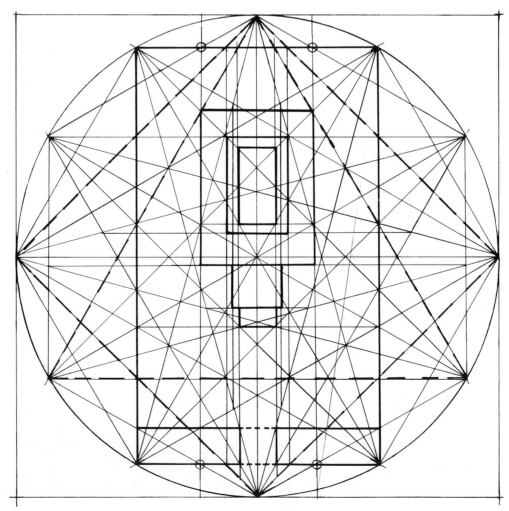

Figure 84b

The distances used to position the central bark-chapel are equal to the hypotenuse of the Osiris triangle (see Figure 83b). The external width and the internal diagonal of this bark-chapel are equal to the diagonal of the unit square (see Figure 83b). The remaining outlines in the plan of the temple are related to the diagonal of the double unit square and are indicated by the dotted line in Figure 83c. They run through the points of intersection of the arcs or circles (the radii of these arcs and circles are equal to the diagonal of the double unit square and are centred on the long axis or the long sides of the temple) with the diagonals of the temple, with the diagonals of the constituent double squares (solid, thin lines) and with the hypotenuses of the $\frac{3}{2}:\frac{4}{2}:\frac{5}{2}$ triangles constructed at the corners of the temple behind the bark-chapel (solid, heavy lines).

(b) Peripteral Chapel at El-Kab North (XVIIIth dynasty, 1570–1307 B.C.)[14]

This is a small chapel with the central bark-room surrounded by a pillared peripteros accessible through a front stairway all enclosed within a wall joining the pylon of the entrance (Figure 84a). The grid lines are formed by the inscribed double hexagon (Figure 84b). The width of the temple is equal to the radius of the circle or the side of the inscribed hexagon, and the length of the temple is equal to the height of the hexagon. The width of the pillared peripteros, which is equal to the diagonal (through the external walls) of the bark-room, is defined by the sides of the golden rectangles. It can be seen that the thickness of the walls of the bark-room, the peripteros and of the pylon are not chosen arbitrarily but depend on definite points of intersection within the grid.

(c) Tomb of Rameses IV (XXth dynasty, c. 1140 B.C.)

Figure 86a is part of the ancient plan of the tomb from an original drawing on papyrus, showing the burial chamber and the sarcophagus surrounded by six concentric enclosures. The grid of the analysis (Figure 85b) is shown in Figures 81a and b. The arcs are centred on the points of intersection of the sides of the circumscribed square with the sides (heavy dotted lines) of the golden rectangles, and their radius is equal to one half the diagonal of the golden rectangles. The sarcophagus, the inner and outer lines of the walls of the first enclosure have been traced, and only the outer lines of these walls of the second, third, fourth and sixth enclosures and the corners of the fifth enclosure have been indicated at the lower end of the sarcophagus.

The burial chamber is off square. The outer wall of the width of the sixth enclosure and the inner walls of the third enclosure are defined by the sides of the golden rectangles. The outer walls along the length of the sixth enclosure are limited by the centres of the golden rectangles. The outer walls (including those not traced) are drawn through the points of intersection of the diagonals of the golden rectangles or the diameters of the circle with the arcs of the grid. The lower end of the sarcophagus is placed on the centre of the circle and the centre of the upper golden rectangle is situated above the head of the Pharaoh where the crown begins.

This analysis of the tomb of Rameses IV differs from that carried out by Hambidge[15] who presented a plan of the tomb, which referred to only three concentric 'sarcophagi', the innermost measuring a double square-shape which could not be verified on the plan used here. Since Egyptians believed in building in accordance with the 'divine order' of the universe, the seven enclosures or walls about the mummy may relate to the seven planets, the seven days of the week or the seven 'plumettes' of Sefkhet, the goddess of 'builders and books'.

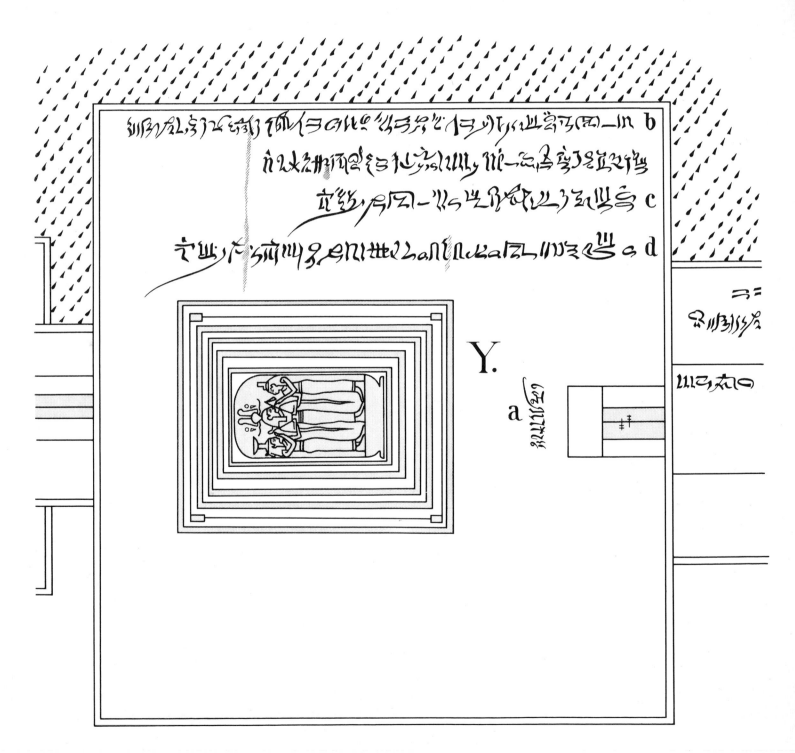

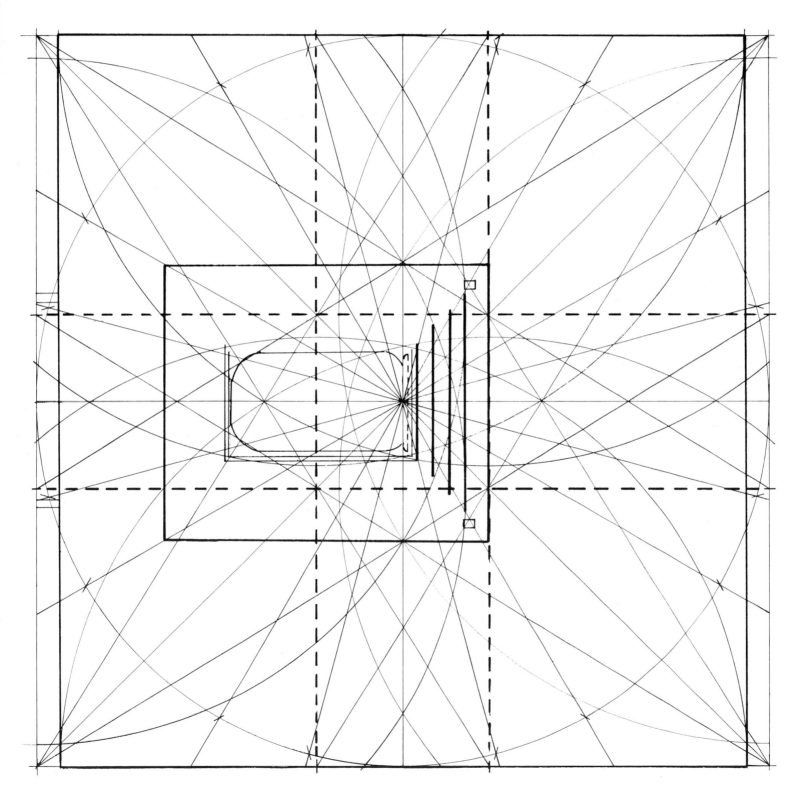

3 Building According to the 'Divine Order of the Universe'

The Egyptian triangle of Osiris[16] may have gained its 'divine significance' not only in containing a right angle but also on account of its two sides and hypotenuse being measurable in rational numbers or units, i.e., 3, 4 and 5, respectively, adding up to 12, the key unit of the Egyptian mensuration system. As we said before, the Ancient Egyptians had made an attempt to use the fraction, the numerator of which was always equal to one,

$\frac{1}{4}, \frac{1}{5}, \frac{1}{8}$, etc., and the difference of the fraction from unity, e.g., $\frac{3}{4}, \frac{4}{5}, \frac{7}{8}$, respectively, was represented as a subtraction from unity, e.g.,

$1 - \frac{1}{4}, 1 - \frac{1}{5}, 1 - \frac{1}{8}$, respectively. The only exception to this rule was the $\frac{2}{3}$, which was referred to by a special term and represented by the symbol ⊤.[17]

The $\frac{2}{3}$ may be a reference to $\frac{8}{12}$, eight being the sum of the hypotenuse and the short side of the Osiris triangle and/or may represent the peculiar geometric relationship between the Osiris triangle and the generation of the 1:2 right-angled triangle. The dimensions of all types of triangles shown to be used in Egyptian architectural planning (see page 116) are related to the dimensions of the Osiris triangle. In Figure 86 the sides of the right-angled triangle ACD are in the ratio of 1:2 (therefore related to the rectangle of sides 1:2, which we mentioned to be of significance in Egyptian architectural planning) and the sides of the right-angled triangle CDE are in the ratio of 3:4, i.e., the 3:4:5 Osiris triangle. The side AC of the right-angled triangle ACD is sectioned (see Figure 59 for method) by point B such that

$\frac{AC}{AB} = \frac{AB}{BC} = \phi$ where AB = 4.99 ≐ 5.0, and

therefore AB + EC ≐ AC(8.0). The number eight might thus have gained a significance for the Egyptians who wished to build in the 'divine order'. Numbers 3, 5 and 8 are included in the Fibonacci series[18], and $\frac{5}{3} ≐ \frac{8}{5} ≐ \phi$ (see page 82).

'The Divinity' in the relationship of these numbers may, therefore, date from the time of the Ancient Egyptians. The monuments analysed above were erected a few centuries apart over a period of about eight centuries. In the temple of Sesostris I, the central bark-chapel, i.e., the holy area, was proportioned using the hypotenuse of the Osiris triangle. Later, the chapel in the temple of El-Kab and the burial chamber of Rameses IV were both designed by the use of the ϕ proportioning system. There is evidence that the Egyptians did keep 'archives' which may be the 'books' guarded by Sefkhet, hidden in the temple chambers and containing the 'secrets' of the ancient plans for building in the divine order, only accessible to the Pharaoh and the appointed men of proper skills.[19] The 'divine' methods of building may have started by the use of the triangle of Osiris, and the more sophisticated geometric method of proportioning with ϕ as described on pages 82 to 83 may have occurred later with development of knowledge and skills in geometry and planning.

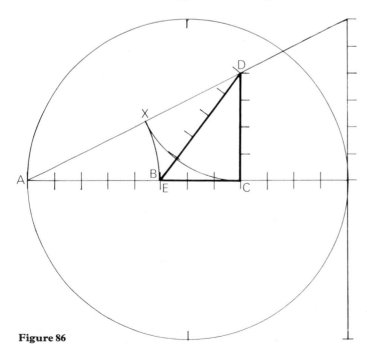

Figure 86

4 Islamic Concepts in Architecture

Architectural styles, distinguished by architectural forms, are determined by principles in design and in the usage of building materials; the 'formulae' and the 'media' of their application reflect the knowledge and beliefs of a society. For example, the Ancient Egyptians who believed in immortality used mostly stone, despite the abundance of the much more easily workable mud, from the Old Kingdom 3100 B.C. until the death of Cleopatra at the end of the Ptolemaic period 30 B.C., whereas the Mesopotamians, e.g., the Sumerians and Assyrians who believed in finite existence, used only mud brick. Similarly, in the Roman world irrespective of the variations in the local availability of building materials, specific architectural forms were always constructed with the same 'formulae' and 'media'. In the Muslim world, which spread wider than the Roman Empire, both the formulae and the media were determined by the local conditions and traditions, such that at least six principal styles, Syro-Egyptian, Mesopotamian and Persian, Andalusian and North African, Turkish, Indo-Islamic and South Arabian have evolved. The mosque is the most prominent example of the types of Islamic architecture which include the fort, palace, *khān* or *caravanserai*, *madrasah* (school), hospital, hostels for poor, closed bazaar, *ḥammam* (public baths), mausoleum, fountain, etc. The mosque is an enclosure for prayer and consists of: the *saḥn* (a courtyard where the fountain for ablution is placed); the sanctuary or the sheltered area with the *miḥrab* (a niche in a wall indicating the direction of Mecca), the *mimbar* (elevated pulpit) of the Imam (the leader of the congregation) and the minaret. There is, however, no standardized or basic plan determining the relative positions or the proportions of these component structures, nor a preference for specific building material. Indeed, the forms of the domes, arches and minarets vary radically from North Africa to Turkey and India (see Plates 41–46).

The decoration of the exteriors and interiors of Islamic buildings and monuments was predominantly non-representational and, in the case of the mosque, invariably so. Calligraphy and geometric designs were used to convey an effect appropriate to the purpose of the buildings. The concepts and the method with which the architect and the designer worked were the same, enabling them to achieve a totality of purpose in artistic creation.

5 Planning

The analysis of the plans of three mosques and three palaces from different regions of the Muslim world have been presented below in chronological order. It can be seen that the best grid lines of analysis were in each case based on the square and the $\sqrt{2}$ system of proportioning (see page 8). As we said before, the creations of man reflect his beliefs, and the methodology borrowed from previous civilizations, from the common human heritage, is developed to suit the practices and purposes of a particular society. We suggested that the earliest traceable origins of Islamic methods of architectural planning may have been in Ancient Egypt. However, as the methods of Egyptians were relevant to their particular interpretation of the universal order, so methods appear to have been adopted to suit the Islamic perspective. In the fifth epistle of the Ikhwān al-Ṣafā',[20] it has been explained at length that 'God has created in his wisdom this universe engendered with mortality in squares (or fours) consisting of compatible and opposing (or incompatible) pairs. The secrets of which are only known to their Creator'.[21] The statement 'and of everything we have created pairs' was also quoted by them from the Quran (LI, 49) in support of this theory. It has been proposed, for example, that one of each of the four seasons of the year, of the four quarters of the day, of the lunar month, of the Zodiac signs, of the four directions of the compass and the four winds from these directions, of the four elements and the four physical properties, of the four humours, the four ages, moralities and behaviours of man, of the four types of sensations, of smell, and of taste, of the four preferences for colour and musical sounds, and of the four strings of the lute, one of each of these fall into the same category; thus 'all living beings and the objects in this world fall into four categories'.[22] 'When the compatible combine in right proportions, they potentiate each other's effects and overcome their opposites.'[23] 'This is the way wise men prepare their curing remedies'[24] (which is reminiscent of the Ancient Egyptian way of balancing health versus illness). Therefore, one could argue that there was a conviction at the foundation of Islamic methodology or architectural planning. The basic grid upon which the plans were designed imparted the unity, but the freedom in choice of the design allowed for the artistic creativity and the development of regional or local styles.

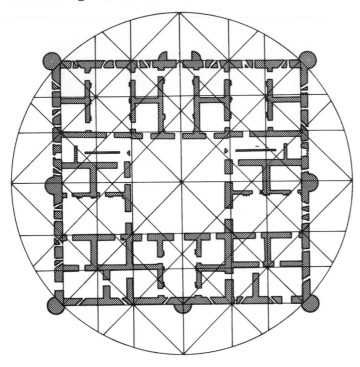

Figure 87. Qasr al-Kharānah, Jordan, 1st/7th century. Plan of upper floor.

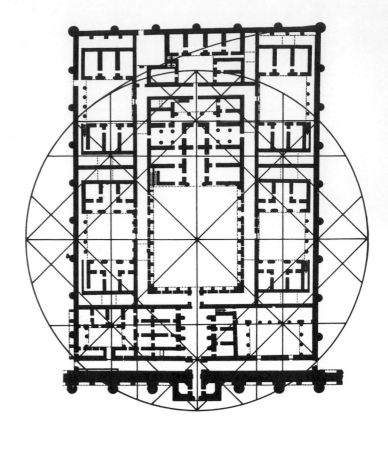

Figure 89. Ukhayḍir, near Baghdad, 158/775.

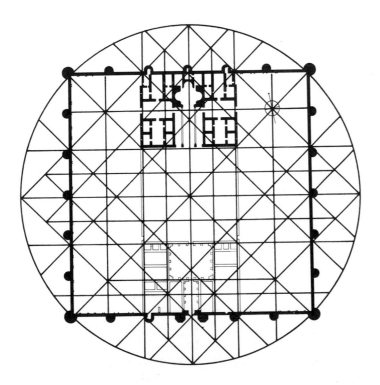

Figure 88. Mshattā, Syria, 132/750.

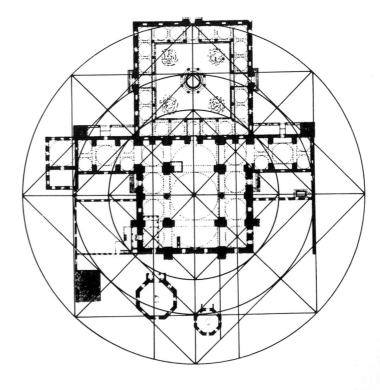

Figure 90. Mosque of Bāyezīd II, Bursa, Turkey, 906/1501.

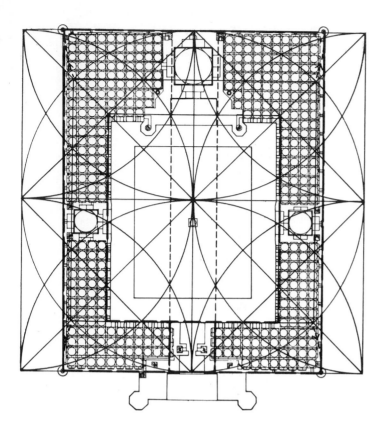

Figure 91. Tomb of Bībī Khānum, Samarqand, USSR, 800–806/1398–1404.

Figure 92. Tomb of I'timād al-Dawla, Agra, India, 1037/1628.

References

1. Badawy, A., *Ancient Egyptian Architectural Design*, p. 4.

2. Budge, E. A. W., pp. 424, 426.

3. Badawy, A., *op. cit.*, pp. 58–60.

4. Badawy, A., *op. cit.*, pp. 8–9.

5. Badawy, A., *op. cit.*, p. 46.

6. Badawy, A., *op. cit.*, pp. 5–9.

7. Badawy, A., *op. cit.*, pp. 8–9.

8. Chambers Encyclopaedia, see *Measure*.

9. Erman, A., pp. 365–8.

10. Badawy, A., *op. cit.*, pp. 2, 23, 24.

11. Badawy, A., *op. cit.*, p. 85.

12. Badawy, A., *op. cit.*, pp. 23, 25.

13. Badawy, A., *op. cit.*, p. 23.

14. Badawy, A., *op. cit.*, p. 97.

15. Ghyka, M., p. 41.

16. Badawy, A., *op. cit.*, p. 23.

17. Erman, A., pp. 365–8.

18. Badawy, A., *op. cit.*, p. 4.

19. Badawy, A., *op. cit.*, pp. 5–9.

20. Ikhwān al-Ṣafā', Vol. I, pp. 229–32.

21. Ikhwān al-Ṣafā', Vol. I, pp. 229–32.

22. Ikhwān al-Ṣafā', Vol. I, pp. 229–32.

23. Ikhwān al-Ṣafā', Vol. I, pp. 229–32.

24. Ikhwān al-Ṣafā', Vol. I, pp. 229–32.

Plate 41. Sayyidah Nafīsah Mosque, Cairo, 13th/19th century.
Plate 42. Malwīya, the Great Mosque, Sāmarrā, Iraq, 9th/15th century.
Plate 43. Madrasah-yi Mādar-i Shāh, Isfahan, Iran.
Plate 44. Sidi Bu Medien, Tlemcen, Algeria.
Plate 45. Sulṭān Aḥmed Mosque, Istanbul, Turkey.
Plate 46. Quṭb Minār, Delhi, India.

Plate 41

Plate 42

Plate 43

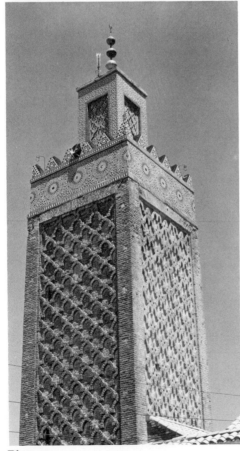

Plate 44

Plate 45

Plate 46

Chapter IV
Arabic Calligraphy

Calligraphy in Arabic is referred to as *handasat al-khaṭṭ* (the geometry of line), 'line' meaning 'letters' or 'writing'. Since the rise of Islam, calligraphy has been a major art form. Numerous manuscripts have survived describing new methods of writing and combining different scripts, and also explaining diligently the shaping and proportioning of letters, the making and manipulation of pens for each script, and the preparation of colours, inks and paper.

In the early Islamic period there were two main types of writing, *al-kūfī al-yābis* (dry Kufic), which was angular and rigid, and *al-kūfī al-layyin* (soft Kufic) also called *al-kūfī al-muqawwar* (rounded Kufic). The latter, although characterized by strong angularity, also incorporated rounded elements and can be identified as the prototype of the later 'Cursive Scripts'. The cursive scripts have also been called the *naskh* scripts (*naskh* meaning copy) because of the fluency of transcribing achieved by using the rounded forms of letters. Arabic calligraphers referred to the smooth style of writing with rounded letters as adding humidity (*ruṭūbah*) to a script so as to moisten its characteristic dryness or angularity. The *naskh* scripts should not be confused with the 'Nashkī Script' which is a distinct style in the *naskh* or cursive scripts. Therefore, in this chapter, the *naskh* scripts are referred to as the cursive scripts. In the course of time there evolved from these two early Kufic scripts many different styles of writing including those now used in the Muslim world.

By the tenth century A.D., floriate, foliated, plaited and many other Kufic styles had developed from the angular Kufic script, which was especially used in architectural decorations, the manuscripts of the Quran, and inscriptions on coins. The Maghribī (Western) script, with its differing forms in Andalusia, Fez, Kairouan and elsewhere and still used in North Africa, was established by introducing stylistic variations into the original Kufic. The essential angularity was preserved but the ordering of the letters in the alphabet and the forms of indicating the letters *fā'* and *qāf* by dots (see below) were different from the cursive Mashriqī (Eastern) scripts.

	letter *fā'*	letter *qāf*
Maghribī	ف	ڢ
Mashriqī	ق	ف

The Cursive Scripts

It is claimed that the distinguished Abbasid *wazīr* (minister) and calligrapher Ibn Muqlah[1] (d. 327/939) was the first to have developed a geometric method of construction and proportioning the Arabic letters in the cursive scripts.

The thickness of the line drawn by the pen employed was the unit measure for the size of the letters, and was referred to as the *nuqṭah* (point). The proportion of the thickness to the length of the letter *alif* (the first letter of the Arabic alphabet, and written as a vertical straight line) determined the basis of construction of the script. When a circle was drawn with the *alif* as diameter, the shape and the proportional sizes of all the other letters of the alphabet could be derived from this circle, as will be shown later. The system of *nisbah faḍīlah* (noble proportion) of calligraphy, based on the method of Ibn Muqlah was outlined in one of the fifty-two epistles written in Basra at the end of the tenth century A.D. by the Ikhwān al-Ṣafā'[2] (Brethren of Purity – who aimed at integrating Islamic and Greek philosophies). The proportion of the thickness to the length of the *alif* was 1:8 points (Figure 93a). The letters *bā'*, *tā'*, and *tha*, which differ only in the number and position of indication dots, were equal to the *alif*,

i.e., eight points long (Figure 93c). Letters with rounded forms were equal to one-half or one-quarter of the circumference of the circle drawn with the *alif* as the diameter. Therefore, for convenience of explanation, the circumference of this circle is equalled to twenty-four points (Figure 93b), although mathematically, the circumference $d\pi$ is equal to $25\frac{1}{7}$ points. The upper stroke of the letters *jīm*, *ḥā'* or *khā'*, which also differ with respect to the indication dots, was four points (one-half of the length of the *alif*), and the lower arc was one-half of the circumference of the circle or twelve points (Figure 93d).

The letters *rā'* or *zā'*, without and with an indication dot, respectively, were each one-quarter of the circumference of the circle, i.e., six points long (Figure 93e). The other letters of the alphabet were constructed with similar reference to the *alif* and the circle.

All cursive scripts which have developed since Ibn Muqlah have been constructed by this same geometric method based on the *alif* and the circle; they differ in the length of the *alif*, and the relative proportions of the other letters to the *alif* or its circle.

The Thuluth was one of the first scripts based on the method of Ibn Muqlah. It may have been called Thuluth (one-third) because the proportion of a diameter to the circumference of its circle is one to π, which is slightly less than one-third. In this script, the proportion of the width to the length of the *alif* was seven points. In the Naskhī Script and the Ruq'ah Script the length of the *alif* was six and three points respectively. Differences in the construction of various scripts include, amongst others, the inclinations of the vertical and horizontal elements of the letters, the roundness of the curved forms and the decorative treatment of vowel signs (Figure 94).[3]

Figure 93

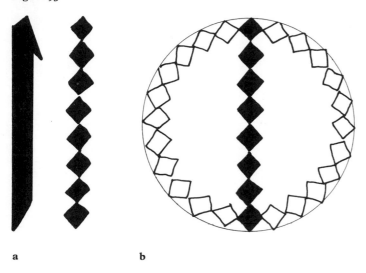

a   b

c

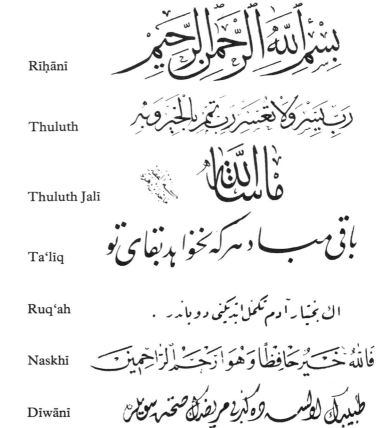

Rīḥānī

Thuluth

Thuluth Jalī

Ta'līq

Ruq'ah

Naskhī

Diwānī

Figure 94. From Zayn al-Din.[3]

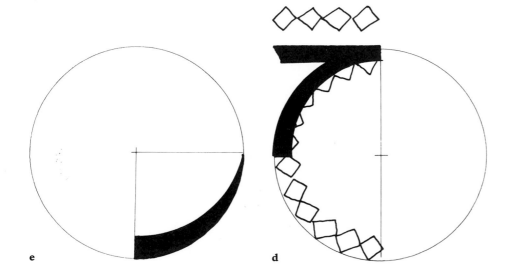

e   d

From the Abbasid period onwards the Arabic alphabet was adapted to other languages, such as Persian, Seljuk and Ottoman Turkish, Hindustani, Pushtu, Malay, Berber and Swahili. The Ta'liq or Naskhi Ta'liq Script was developed in Persia in the eleventh century A.D., and the Diwānī Scripts were developed in Turkey in the mid-fifteenth century and were used as the official scripts of the Ottoman Empire. With the invention of these different cursive scripts, calligraphy developed into a major decorative art form which provided scope for self-expression to the artist in the Muslim world.

Figure 95. The hexagonal, octagonal and pentagonal stars (which were shown in Chapter II to be master grids of the design) may in this case have had a mystical significance since they have been associated with the name of the Prophet Mohammad and 'Allah' (which is placed centrally, see Figures 95b and c) and positioned at the centre of the dome or vault.

Figure 95a. Dome of the Ulu Cami, Eski Malatya, Turkey, 645/1247.

Figure 95b. Vault in mausoleum of Öljeitü, Sulṭāniyya, Iran, early 8th/14th century.

Figure 95c. Vault in mausoleum of Öljeitü, Sulṭāniyya, Iran, early 8th/14th century.

References

1. Zayn al-Dīn, N., p. 96.

2. Ikhwān al-Ṣafā', Vol. I, pp. 220–1.

3. Zayn al-Dīn, N., fig. 404 on p. 127.

Chapter V
The Circles of
'*Arūḍ* in Arabic Poetry

Arabic literature of the Jāhilīyah or the pre-Islamic period had been developed to a high degree of perfection. The annual meetings at the commercial fair of 'Ukāẓ were renowned as literary arenas where poets demonstrated their skills. The *mu'allaqāt*, the seven odes of pre-Islamic Arabia, were so highly regarded that they were hung in the Kaaba. These poems were in themselves sufficient proof of the remarkable achievement of the Arabic language. Poetry was highly formalized, governed by strict rules which were not documented, and, therefore, the metre as well as the quality of the poem was assessed by the trained ear. Arabic poetry was rarely recorded, but transmitted orally through each generation.

Al-Khalīl ibn Aḥmad, born 99/718, is accepted as the first Arab philologist to have systematically categorized the metres of classical Arabic poetry into fifteen distinct types. Later his student Al-Akhfash added the sixteenth and final type of metre.

Al-Khalīl standardized the use of eight words called the Tafi'lah (comparable to metrical feet, and which will be referred to as verbal units) such that the repetition of one or two, but not more, verbal units in a particular coded order produced the metre of a line of verse. The system of the Tafi'lah, together with other strict rules, not elaborated here but referred to by Al-Khalīl as the 'circles of 'arūḍ' ('arūḍ meaning the science of making poetry), provided the means to scan Arabic poetry and to classify it into its sixteen metres.

In the Arabic language vowels are indicated by three signs, the *fatḥah*, *ḍammah* and *kasrah*, written above or below each letter and called the *ḥarakāt* (motions). The absence of a vowel is indicated by the *sukūn* (silent) sign above a letter. The three *madd* letters, *alif*, *waw* and *yā*, which in the ordinary language are either long vowels or consonants, have a special function in the Tafi'lah system; they are always considered consonants with the silent sign. Thus, a series of letters with their vowels and silent signs constitutes a verbal unit which, when repeated in a particular order, dictates the order of the vowels and silents in a line of verse and thereby determines the phonetic pattern. The poet has to choose his words such that the successive vowels and consonants in the line of poetry coincide with those of the chosen phonetic pattern. In the diagrammatic presentation of the verbal unit, the vowel and silent signs, i.e., 'sub-units' of each verbal unit, are indicated by the vertical stroke and the circle, respectively:

Verbal Unit		Sub-units
fa 'u W lu n	فَعُولُنْ	I I O I O
ma fa A 'i Y lu n	مَفَاعِيلُنْ	I I O I O I O

The capital letters (the *madd* letters *alif*, *waw* and *yā*) indicate silences. Each underlined letter or letters of the verbal unit is represented by the sub-units placed in the same order as these letters.

The scanning of classical Arabic poetry by sub-units thus uses a quantitative and not a syllabic system. For example, in the unmodified form of the Ṭawīl (long) metre, which came to be the most popular of the sixteen coded metres of Arabic verse, two verbal units, *fa 'u W lu n, ma fa A 'i Y lu n* فَعُولُنْ مَفَاعِيلُنْ are repeated alternately four times with a result that the forty-eight sub-units (see Table I) establish the characteristic rhythm of each line.

Table I

Ṭawīl Metre (in sub-units)

I I O I O I I O I O I O I I O I O I I O I O I O X I I O I O I I O I O I O I I O I O I I O I O I O

The ratios of the number of vowels to silent signs in the whole, in one-half and in one-quarter of the Ṭawīl metre are 28:20, 14:10 and 7:5, respectively. It is this geometric proportioning of the sub-units which gives the poetry its *mīzān* (order and balance).

In the Arabic poem each line has a complete meaning of its own, and is always constructed in the same metre. Each line can be shown, therefore, to bear the same relationship to the whole of the poem as the repeat pattern to the overall design (as discussed in Chapter II). The construction of the metre based on one verbal unit repeated eight times (e.g., Mutaqārib and Mutadārik metres) or two successive verbal units repeated four times (e.g. Ṭawīl and Basīṭ metres) can be compared to the construction of the repeat pattern on the master grid of the octagonal star (Figures 96a and b respectively). Similarly, construction of the metre based on one verbal unit repeated six times (e.g., Ramal and Kāmil metres), or two successive verbal units repeated three times (e.g., Khafīf metre) can be compared to the construction of the repeat pattern on the master grid of the hexagonal star (Figure 96c and d, respectively). In the case of Figure 96b and d, the two inscribed polygons may have any relative positions except for superimposition. The example of all the sixteen metres of classical Arabic can be used to form the master grids based on the octagonal or hexagonal stars[1] as illustrated in Figure 96. The construction of the metre or the phonetic pattern for a line of verse from vowels and consonants combined in definite proportion and sequence by the use of the same or two different types of verbal units is comparable to the construction of a particular master grid and hence to the repeat pattern of a design from constituent polygonal units positioned at definite angles to each other by the use of equal or proportional segments of the circumscribing circle. In other words the same concept determines the making of rhythm in space or rhythm in time.

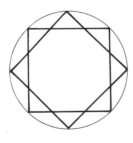
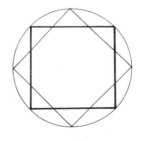

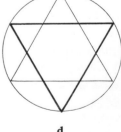

a   b   c   d

Figure 96

Reference

1. Ṣammūd, N., p. 20.

Chapter VI
Music in the Muslim World

The early theory of classical Arabic music is the same as that of the *mīzān* of Arabic poetry (see Chapter V) from which music making developed as an orally transmitted (i.e., undocumented) art form. The cultural exchange in the Muslim world established this theory as the common basis of independent music making also in Persia, Turkey and North Africa. In the early Islamic period (seventh and eight centuries A.D.) singers like Ṭuways, Ibn Muḥriz and Ibn Misjaḥ (the latter under the patronage of the Umayyad Khalifate in Damascus) travelled extensively in Persia and the Byzantine countries acquainting themselves with the local music which they modified to suit their own rhythms. Ibn Misjaḥ is believed to be one of the earliest musicians to record the theory of classical Arabic music in the Muslim world. In the eighth century A.D., the Ṣinā'at al-Mūsīqā (the craft of music making) was described by musicians like Zalzal and Al-Muṣillī. Later philosophers like Al-Kindī (ninth century A.D.) introduced methods of systematic analysis and coding based on the Hellenic theories of music which Euclid, Aristoxenus and Nichomachos had developed. Music became so highly regarded that a vast literature on the history of poetry and music was accumulated, of which *Al-'Aqd al-Farīd* by Ibn 'Abd Rabbih (b. 246/860), and the *Kitāb al-Aghānī* in twenty-one volumes by Al-Isfahānī (d. 356/967) are the best known.

The Construction of Classical Arabic Music

In the fifth epistle by the Ikhwān al-Ṣafā' (see page 125), the rules of musical composition were developed from the *mīzān* of poetry.[1] Early Arabic music therefore consisted of singing lines of verse with rhythmic accompaniment determined by the *mīzān* of the poetry. Purely instrumental music, a later development, was also governed by the rules of vocal music. (Although contemporary western scholars of eastern music may find the Ikhwān al-Ṣafā' unrepresentative of the later developments in these rules, we choose to refer to this earlier source since the later changes were not fundamental deviations from the principles described here.)

(a) Rhythm

The three basic rhythmic sub-units of Arabic music are made up from the same sub-units as the verbal units of the Tafi'lah system of poetry (see Table 2) and are described below. The notation of sub-units of the Tafi'lah system are included here to compare these with the smallest musical elements, i.e., the musical beats.

Table 2

Type of rhythmic unit	Constituent	By musical beats	Tafi'lah notation
(i) Sabab	one vowel and one silent sign	*tu n*	(10)
(ii) Watad	two vowels and one silent sign	*tu nu n*	(110)
(iii) Fāṣilah	three vowels and one silent sign	*tu nu nu n*	(1110)

The *tu* and *nu* are the syllables representing beats with a sound or without a sound (i.e., a 'rest'), the *tu* being the syllable used to indicate the beginning of a rhythmic unit, and the *n* indicates an infinitesimally short interruption introducing discontinuity of sound, i.e., a break before the next rhythmic unit. The rhythmic units are accented by the strong beat '*dum*' (D), the light beat '*tek*' (T), and the silence or 'rest' *sukūt*' (S), one of which accompanies each musical syllable. The eight principal rhythmic patterns of Arabic music used in the ninth century A.D. (as documented by the Ikhwān al-Ṣafā') are given in Table 4, and, when possible, the rhythmic patterns have been supplemented with typical assignments of musical accents (D, T & S). Variations in the rhythmic patterns and in the accenting, approximately three hundred in all, have developed since the ninth century. These variations are classified into two types, both of which can contain around eighty-eight beats per rhythmic pattern: those containing even numbers of musical beats and those containing odd numbers of musical beats.

Table 3

(1) Al-Thaqil al-Awwal

Tafi'lah	: ma f	'u W	lu n		ma f	ma fa	A 'i Y	lu n		ma f
Tafi'lah notation:	1 0	1 0	1 0		1 0	1 1 0	1 0	1 0		1 0
Musical beats	: tu n	tu n	tu n		tu n	tu nu n	tu n	tu n		tu n
Musical accents	: D	S	T		S	D S	T	S		T
Rhythmic units	: Sabab	Sabab	Sabab		Sabab	Watad	Sabab	Sabab		Sabab

The ratio of 'ḥarakāt' (motions, vowels) to 'sukūns' (un-vowelled silences) or of the number of musical beats to the number of rhythmic units per unit pattern is 9:8. Here *maf* is an interrupted version of *maf'uWlun*. The capital letters in the Tafi'lah indicate un-vowelled silences (the *madd* letters, see page 135).

(2) Khafif al-Thaqil al-Awwal

ma fa	A 'i	l		ma fa	A 'i Y	lu n
1 1 0	1 0			1 1 0	1 0	1 0
tu nu n	tu n			tu nu n	tu n	tu n

(7:5)

(3) Al-Thaqil al-Thānī

ma f	'u W	lu n		ma f	'u W		ma fa	A 'i Y	lu n		ma f	'u W
1 0	1 0	1 0		1 0	1 0		1 1 0	1 0	1 0		1 0	1 0
tu n	tu n	tu n		tu n	tu n		tu nu n	tu n	tu n		tu n	tu n

(11:10)

Here *maf'uW* is another interrupted version of *maf'uWlun*.

(4) Khafif al-Thaqil al-Thānī

fa 'i	lu n		fa 'i	lu n		fa 'i	lu n
1 1 1 0			1 1 1 0			1 1 1 0	
tu nu nu n			tu nu nu n			tu nu nu n	

(9:3)

(5) Al-Ramal

fa A	'i lu n		ma fa	A 'i	lu n
1 0	1 1 0		1 1 0	1 0	1 0
tu n	tu nu n		tu n	tu nu n	
D	S T		D S		T T

(7:4)

(6) Khafif al-Ramal

mu ta	fa A	'i la tu n		mu ta	fa A	'i la tu n
1 1 1 0	1 1 1 0			1 1 1 0	1 1 1 0	
tu nu nu n	tu nu nu n			tu nu nu n	tu nu nu n	
D S T		D S T		D S T		T D T

(12:4)

(7) Khafif al-Khafif

ma fa	A 'i	lu n		ma fa	A 'i	lu n
1 1 0	1 0	1 0		1 1 0	1 0	1 0
tu nu n	tu nu	n		tu nu n	tu nu	n
D D	S T			D S		T S

(8:4)

(8) Al-Hazj

fa A	'i lu n		fa A	'i lu n		fa A	'i lu n
1 0	1 1 0		1 0	1 1 0		1 0	1 1 0
tu n	tu nu n		tu n	tu nu n		tu n	tu nu n

(9:6)

The rhythmic pattern is comparable to, and is repeated throughout, a song, like the 'metre' of a line of poetry. As in the making of the 'metre', one type of rhythmic unit is repeated two to four times or two types of rhythmic units are repeated a definite number of times to produce an ordered sequence of beats of the same or different durations, respectively. Since the rhythmic units follow the vowels and consonants of the written word, the use of the appropriate rhythmic pattern enables the transcription of the phonetic rhythm of the line of poetry into music. The ratio of the total number of beats to the verbal units (which is equivalent to the ratio of vowels to the silents and consonants of the line of poetry spanned by the rhythmic pattern) determines the pattern or the sequence of the musical beats, and hence the particular effect of the melody composed on it. A large ratio of beats to units (e.g., pattern nos. 4–7 in Table 3) gives a rhythmic pattern consisting of long beats and provides for longer continuity of sound. A small ratio on the other hand (e.g., nos. 1–3 in Table 3) gives a pattern of small beats repeated many times. The subdivision of the metre of poetry into a sequence of different durations of sound by the use of a definite proportion of beats to verbal units constitutes the geometric basis of the 'craft of music making'.

(b) Melody

The basic musical scale used in the Muslim world consisted of seven notes, forming an octave with the repetition of the first note, as in the western musical scale :

I   yekgāh (rāst)
II   dogah
III segāh
IV   chehargah
V   penjgāh (nawā)
VI   sheshgah (ḥusaynī)
VII haftgāh (awj)
VIII kardān (yekgāh high)

The first, fourth and fifth notes of the scale contained four quarter intervals, i.e., tones (large intervals), and the second, third, sixth and seventh notes contained three quarter intervals (small intervals), the complete scale thus consisting of twenty-four quarter intervals or tones.[2] The large and the small intervals could be shortened or lengthened by the deduction or addition of successive quarter intervals or tones whereby 'chromatic intervals' of, e.g., two or six quarter tones could be formed.

The seven principal *maqāms* (modal scales) of music (Table 4), on which the melody was composed were distinguished by the length of the intervals between the successive seven notes. Variations on each of the seven principal *maqāms* have been found totalling ninety-five different types as listed during the 1932 Arab Music Congress in Cairo.[3] The reader may notice that the 'Ajam *maqām* is identical with the western 'major scale'. The *maqām* was never extended further than two or maximally two and a half octaves in order to make the melody musically appreciable. Each scale had three related 'dimensions' (Table 4).

Table 4

	Intervals in half-tones ($=2$ quarter tones) between the eight notes (the first dimension) of the octave.								Sub-division of the scale in half-tones.			
	(first dimension)								by the fifth (second dimension)		by the fourth (third dimension)	
	I	II	III	IV	V	VI	VII	VIII	I↔V↔VIII		I↔IV↔VIII	
1. 'Ajam	2	2	1	2	2	2	1		7	5	5	7
2. Nāhawand	2	1	2	2	1	3	1		7	5	5	7
3. Rāst	2	1½	1½	2	2	1½	1½		7	5	5	7
4. Bayāt	1½	1½	2	2	1	2	2		7	5	5	7
5. Ṣabā	1½	1½	1	3	1	2	2		7	5	4	8
6. Ḥijāz	1	3	1	2	1½	1½	2		7	5	5	7
7. Sīgāh	1½	2	2	1½	1½	2	1½		7	5	5½	6½

(i) The first dimension is the octave with 12 half-tone intervals between notes I and VIII.
(ii) The second dimension is the subdivision of the scale 'by the fifth' (I↔V↔VIII), in the ratio of 7 : 5 half-tone intervals.
(iii) The third dimension is the subdivision of the scale 'by the fourth' (I↔IV↔VIII), into the ratio of 5 : 7 half-tone intervals (with the exception of the *maqāms* Ṣabā and Sigāh).

It can be seen that the interval between the Vth and the Ist or the Vth and the VIIIth note is always constant (see second dimension, Table 4). This is determined by the 'definite or perfect' effect of 'conclusion' evoked in the human mind when either of the two latter notes are sounded after the Vth. The effect of sounding these notes after the IVth has a slightly less satisfactory sense of conclusion or repose when compared with the effect of the Vth. Since the age of classical Greece, repeated attempts have been made to account for the mathematical significance of these intervals in order to reveal the inherent logic of music. According to Pythagoras, 'The numbers by means of which the agreement of sounds affect our ears with delight are the very same which please our eyes and our minds.'[4] Alberti, the celebrated Renaissance architect, has been quoted as saying that 'harmonic ratios inherent in nature are revealed in music'.[5] (See note, page 140).

(c) Composition

When composing music to poetry, which is still the main form of composing classical music in the Muslim world, the first step is to establish the rhythmic pattern following that of the verse. Then the *maqām* most suitable to the words and the mood of the poetry is chosen, and, finally, the melody is composed to follow this metre and the selected *maqām*. It can be seen that here the rhythmic pattern, or the 'metre' of the song, is the determinant of musical composition, and although a choice of rhythmic patterns, the use of which, requiring advanced musicianship, is available to suit a given metre of poetry, they are nevertheless 'prescribed' or 'set', whereas the 'melody' is subject only to the imagination of the performer/composer. Only those melodies of outstanding originality and beauty came to be documented, but the composers often remained anonymous.

When a cycle or group of songs is being composed (or performed), it is customary to present together those composed on the same *maqām*. The effect of repetitiousness, which could be imparted to the songs as a result of the limited choice of rhythmic patterns used with a given *maqām*, is overcome mainly by the changes in melody, the order of the musical accents (which alters the intonation) and by the speed of the performance. In the Andalusian school of singing, for example, the speed of the performance moves from slow to fast and prepares the listeners for the finale of a particular section. Change in mood from one group of poems to the next necessitates a skilful 'passage' from the previous to the new *maqām*. The smoothness and beauty of this transition depends entirely on the creativity and the musicianship of the performer, and may be compared to the cadenzas rendered by European instrumentalists. The 'passage phase' as it is called, is achieved almost like 'modulation' in western music, by going through the scales of *maqāms* of common notes and intervals and finally homing in on the desired *maqām*. Song cycles often begin and end in the same *maqām* to render a unity to the whole performance which may have spanned a number of different *maqāms* as dictated by the changing moods or topics introduced in the cycle.

In apprenticeship, acquisition of the knowledge of the relationships of the different rhythmic patterns and *maqāms*, the skills of applying musical rhythmic units to the metre of poetry and of playing the musical instruments are emphasized equally. The achievement of perfect musicianship lies in this synthesis and is judged by the fluency and spontaneity of the musician in composing/improvising. It is this craftsmanship which forms the common basis of music making in the Muslim world. Distinct styles, e.g. Turkish, Persian, North African, etc., have been developed by the introduction of variations on the basic rhythmic patterns and *maqāms* to suit the differences of language or dialect, and the poetry of the different regions. In the Muslim world we can thus equate the 'craftsman-designer' with the 'craftsman-musician' (or with the poet) who improvises on rhythmic guidelines in the creation of musical (or phonetic) designs.

Note

When we apply the Fibonacci series, which approximates ϕ by the proportion $\frac{3}{2} \simeq \frac{5}{3} \simeq \frac{8}{5} \simeq \frac{13}{8}$ ($\simeq \phi$), also described on page 82, to the notes of the Ajām *maqām* over a span of two octaves by equating note I to number 1 of the Fibonacci series and the successive notes at half-tone intervals after note I to the numbers 2, 3, 4, 5, 6, etc., of this series, the numbers 1, 5, 8 and 13 of the series correspond to the notes I, III, V and VIII, respectively, which are perfectly harmonious notes belonging to what is musically described as the overtones of note I.

References

1. Ikhwān al-Ṣafā', Vol. I, p. 227.

2. Hāfudh, M. M., pp. 180–9.

3. Hāfudh, M. M., pp. 180–9.

4. Wittkower, R., p. 110.

5. Wittkower, R., p. 110.

Chapter VII
Analyses of Patterns in the Applied Arts

In this chapter detailed analyses of various designs in the applied arts are presented to illustrate how patterns and proportion have been derived geometrically.

Figure 97

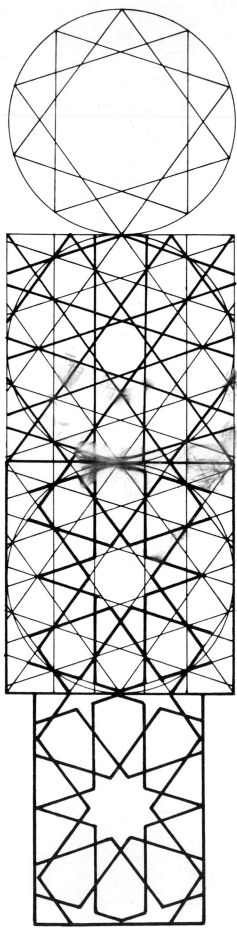

Plate 47. Inlaid panel from door, Cairo, Egypt, probably 8th/14th century.

Figure 98

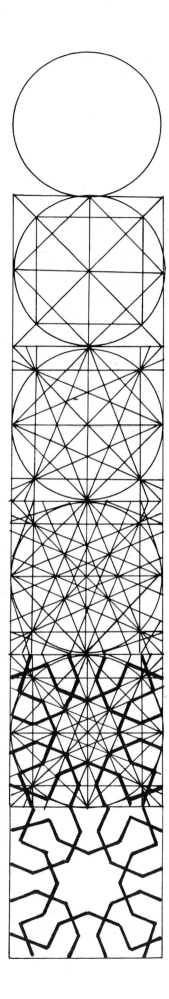

Plate 48. Glazed tiles, Bukhara, USSR, 8th/14th century.

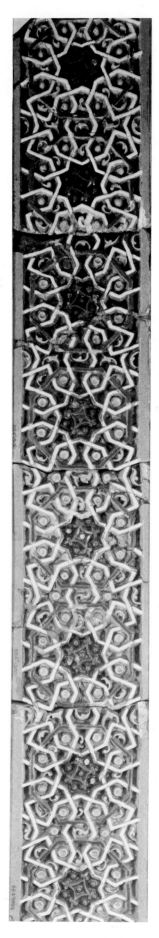

Plate 49. Tiles from the Great Mosque, Damascus, Syria, 8th–9th/14th–15th century.

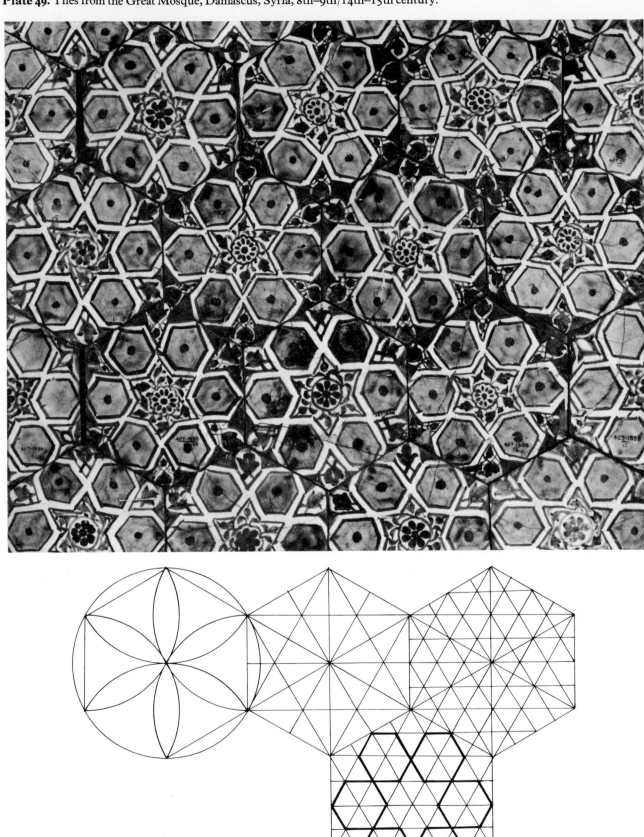

Figure 99

144

Plate 50. Bowl, Samarqand type, 3rd/9th century.

Figure 100

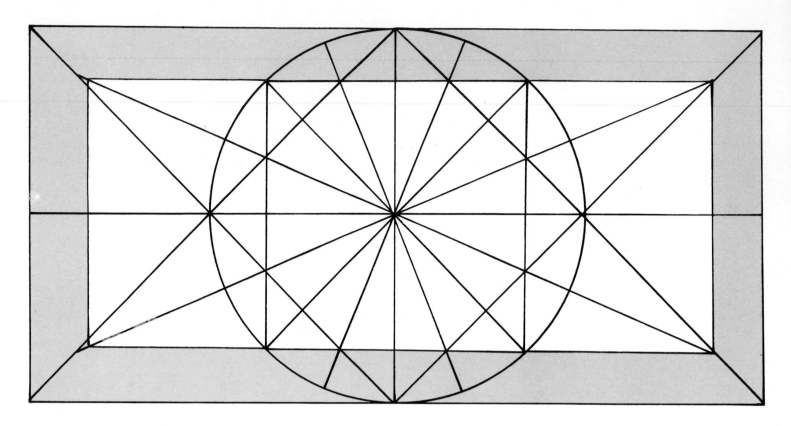

Plate 51. The Ardabil carpet, Tabriz, 946/1539.

Figure 101

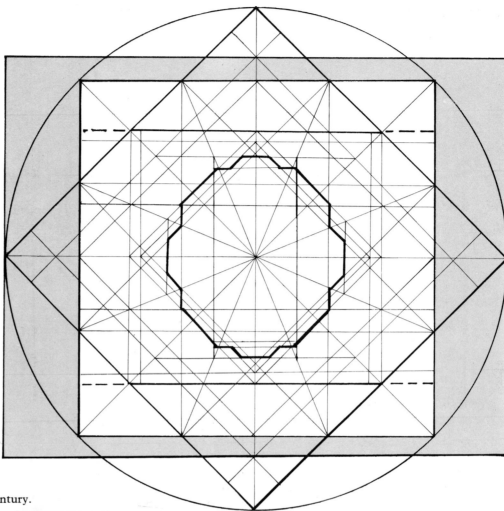

Plate 52. Carpet, Cairo, Egypt, 10th/16th century.

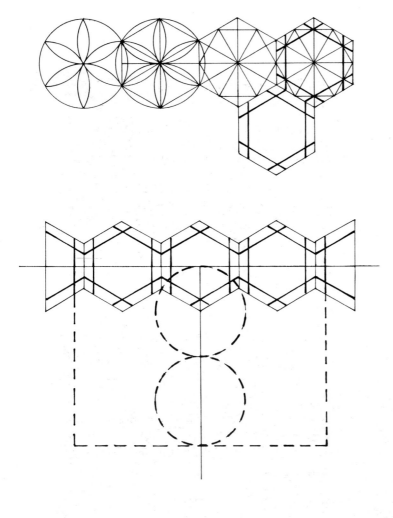

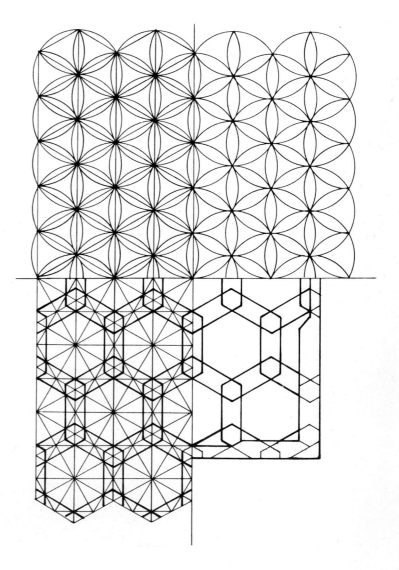

Figure 102c

Plate 53. Quran. Mosul, Iraq 8th/14th century.

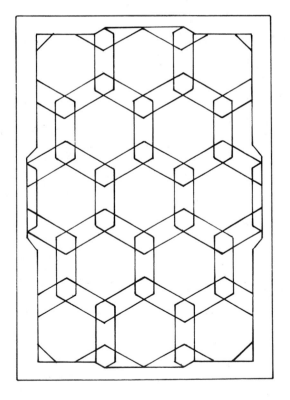

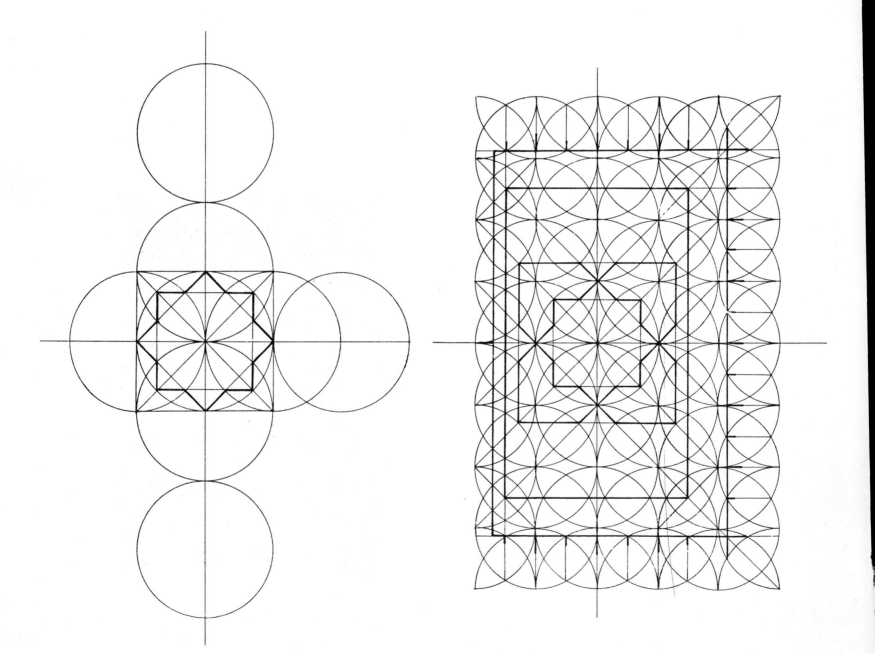

Figure 103c

Plate 54. Quran, Egyptian, 8th/14th century.

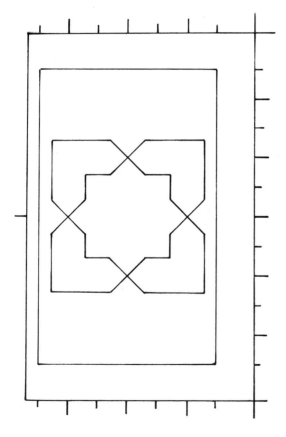

Conclusion

With the expansion of Islam, Arabic, the language of the Quran became the cultural language of the Muslim world. During the ninth century A.D., with the development of educational institutions in cities such as Baghdad and Merv, works of alien cultures, for example, Greek, Indian, Turkish and Persian, in the fields of music, mathematics, astronomy, natural sciences, medicine and philosophy, which had so far been translated only into Syriac, were studied systematically, developed and documented in Arabic. This trend produced the 'universal man' of the Muslim world – Al-Kindī, Al-Fārābī (Alpharabius), Ibn Sīnā (Avicenna), Ibn Bājja (Avempace), Ibn Rushd (Averroes) of the ninth, tenth, eleventh and twelfth centuries, respectively – whose works were translated into Latin. The making of a man who was a scientist, musician, mathematician, astronomer, lawyer, etc., all in one was made possible by applying a methodical approach to studying and writing in the fields of sciences and arts, which aimed to deepen the understanding of the order of the universe and thereby establish a way of life harmonious with it. Therefore, in its openness or its 'evolutionary' disposition, the Islamic tradition in sciences and arts has achieved a continuity of the common human heritage. The adoption and application of a geometrical method as a unifying basis to diverse fields of self-expression is one such contribution which we have attempted to emphasize in this book.

He hath created man
He hath taught him power of expression
The sun and the moon are made punctual . . .

And the sky He hath uplifted;
And He hath set the balance
That ye exceed not the balance
But observe it strictly, nor fall short thereof.

(Quran, Sūrah LV, The Beneficent)

153

Bibliography

Albarn, K. *The Language of Pattern*, London, 1974.

Ardalan, N. *The Sense of Unity*, Chicago, 1973.

Badawy, A. *Ancient Egyptian Architectural Design*, University of California Press, 1965.
A History of Egyptian Architecture, Vol. I, Cairo, 1954.
Al-Bayrūni, A. M. *The Elements of the Art of Astronomy*, London, 1934.

Bennett, I. *Oriental Carpets and Rugs*, London, 1972.

Bourgoin, J. *Arabic Geometrical Pattern and Design*, New York, 1973.

Bronowski, J. *The Ascent of Man*, London, 1974.

Budge, E. A. W. *The Gods of the Egyptians*, Vols I and II, New York, 1969.

Christie, A. H. *Pattern Design*, New York, 1929.

Creswell, K. A. C. *Early Muslim Architecture*, Vol. I, Oxford, 1969.

Critchlow, K. *Order in Space*, London, 1973.

Diringer, D. *The Alphabet*, London, 1949.

Du Ry *Art of Islam*, New York, 1920.

Egyptian Publishing Organization *Cairo, 969–1969*, Cairo, 1969.

Erman, A. *Life in Ancient Egypt*, New York, 1971.

Frankfort, H. *The Art and Architecture of the Ancient Orient*, London, 1970.

Gardner, H. *More Mathematical Puzzles and Diversions*, London, 1971.

Ghyka, M. *Geometrical Composition and Design*, London, 1964.

Hāfudh, M. M. *Tārīkh al-Mūsīqā wa'l-Ghinā' al-'Arabī* (History of Arab Music and Song), Cairo.

Hankin, E. H. 'The Drawing of Geometric Patterns in Saracenic Art', *Memoirs of the Archaeological Survey of India, no. 15*, Calcutta, 1925.

Hill, D. & Grabar, O. *Islamic Architecture and its Decorations*, London, 1962.

Al-Ḥilū, S. *Al-Muwashaḥāt al-Andalūsiyyah* (The Songs of Andalusia), Beirut, 1965.

Hogben, C. *Mathematics in the Making*, London, 1960.

Holt, M. *Mathematics in Art*, London, 1971.

Horizon Magazine *Lost Worlds*, London, 1964.

Ikhwān al-Ṣafā' *Rasā'il* (Epistles), edn Beirut, 1957.

Iraqi Engineers Association *Historic Survey of Baghdad*, Baghdad, 1969.

Jensen, H. *Sign, Symbol and Script*, London, 1970.

Lampl, P. *Cities and Planning in the Ancient Near East*, London, n.d.

Lloyd, S. *The Art of the Ancient Near East*, London, 1965.

Pope, A. U. *Persian Architecture*, Oxford, 1971.

Rice, D. T. *Islamic Art*, London, 1965.

Ṣammūd, N. *Al-'Arūḍ al-Mukhtaṣar* (Concise Metrics), Tunis, 1971.

Sawyer, W. W. *Mathematician's Delight*, London, 1969.

Sehen-Thoss, S. & H. *Design and Color in Islamic Architecture*, Washington, 1968.

Skemp, R. *The Psychology of Learning Mathematics*, London, 1971.

Sordo, E. *Moorish Spain*, London, 1971.

Vogt-Goknil, U. *Living Architecture : Ottoman*, London, 1966.

Volwahsen, A. *Living Architecture : Islamic Indian*, London, 1970.

Watt, W. M. *The Majesty That Was Islam*, London, 1974.

Wiet, G. *The Mosques of Cairo*, Paris, 1966.

Wittkower, R. *Architectural Principles in the Age of Humanism*, London, 1967.

Wulff, H. E. *The Traditional Crafts of Persia*, Cambridge, Mass., 1966.

Zayn al-Dīn, N. *Muṣawar al-Khaṭṭ al-'Arabī* (Atlas of Arabic Calligraphy), Baghdad, 1968.